D0707329

Gifts of
Leadership

Gifts of
Leadership

TEAM BUILDING THROUGH FOCUS AND EMPATHY

ART HORN

Published in 1997 by
Stoddart Publishing Co. Limited

Distributed in Canada by
General Distribution Services Inc.
30 Lesmill Road
Toronto, Canada M3B 2T6
Tel. (416) 445-3333
Fax (416) 445-5967
e-mail Customer.Service@ccmailgw.genpub.com

Distributed in the United States by
General Distribution Services Inc.
85 River Rock Drive, Suite 202
Buffalo, New York 14207
Toll-free Tel. 1-800-805-1083
Toll-free Fax 1-800-481-6207
e-mail gdsinc@genpub.com

01   00   99   98   97   1   2   3   4   5

Cataloging in Publication Data
Horn, Arthur H.
Gifts of leadership : team-building through focus and empathy

Includes index.
ISBN 0-7737-5869-0

1. Leadership.   2. Executive ability.   3. Management.   I. Title.

HD57.7.H67 1997   658.4'092   97-930316-8

Cover design: the boy 100
Design and typesetting: Kinetics Design & Illustration

Printed and bound in Canada

To Wally and Joan,
Adam, David, and Melissa

CONTENTS

Gifts of
Leadership

INTRODUCTION

IN fifteen years as a consultant serving managers I have frequently observed how each of us juggles our own goals with our concerns for other people. Finding the right balance between the two is the subject of this book.

You probably know your weaknesses as a manager. And it's likely that many of them can be described in terms of this balancing act. Some managers are so task or goal oriented that they lose sight of other people, which leads to various problems. Others are so open to the people they interact with that they lose sight of their own goals.

At one level, this seems commonsensical and obvious. After all, it's safe to say that all of your thoughts and activities at any given moment are about you and your goals or about other people or things. As you read these words, for example, you are asking yourself either "What's in this for me?" or "What is the idea being discussed here?" In the first case, your attention is on you and in the second, your attention is not. No surprise there.

At another level, however, the challenge is to find the delicate balance while you are in conversation with the people around you. If you are so intent on your goal of getting the job done, for example, you may neglect to pay attention to what others are saying. You may demonstrate that you are not hearing them and, as a result, may not elicit the support you seek to fulfill your own goal. You also may lose out on whatever valuable input they are providing, all because you want what you want.

On the other hand, I have frequently run into managers who lose sight of their own goals because they are so open to the input of others. During conversation they are easily swayed by what their employees are saying. Such a manager might start a conversation designed to find out the status of a task and hear excuses and blame placing so convincing or troubling that the manager just resigns herself to the employee's perspective. Rather than sort out the problems on the spot, she might just give up on her goal and ultimately not get to the root of the problem.

Indeed, a balancing act is required. On a moment-by-moment basis, if we are overly focused on our goals, we reduce our chances of reaching them. And if we are underfocused, we face the same risk.

About half of this book concerns developing your skill at injecting goal-orientation into each moment of your business day. I refer to the tendency to stick with your goals as "focus." Success depends on having a great deal of it; indeed, you probably ended up in management because you already had a fair amount of it. But focus alone can result in undesirable consequences if not counterbalanced by the other broad skill set called empathy. Focus alone will not result in the fulfillment of your goals. Focus and empathy will.

Empathy skills are those that involve paying attention to other people — things like listening, attending to needs and wants, and building relationships. If your empathy skills are high, you are more likely to inspire your troops. They will like you more because they feel that you understand them. By understanding them, you will make better decisions in your effort to reach your goals. Yet in the same way that all focus and no empathy can hurt you badly, having all empathy and no focus can hurt you too. You would be a loving, compassionate manager who serviced people profoundly well but who didn't get anywhere — and cost the organization a fortune in the process. Empathy and focus need to be in balance for us to be optimally effective.

The balance is applicable to managers from a wide range of organizations, large and small, profit-motivated and institutional. I have had the honour of serving as a consultant, coach, trainer, speaker, and educator in a lot of different industries and have further tested its universal applicability. I have described it to large audiences and small groups. I have worked through it as a personal coach with managers from all levels, from frontline supervisors to senior executives, in both union and non-union environments. It's useful to all of us mostly because it concerns communicating with and inspiring people, and it is based on philosophically and academically tight principles.

When you finish this book, your awareness of how to communicate with your team will be broader and more finely tuned. Most people who have digested the ideas report that they make better decisions about how to communicate difficult or challenging things. Like most training, however, the proof is in the practice. Learning these ideas won't guarantee that you will behave any differently; you must make a concerted effort to change what you do.

Whatever change to your leadership style you try to make as a result of reading this book will undoubtedly feel funny or awkward for a while. That is one of the characteristics of learning new behaviours. For example, you might recognize in the book some aspect of your behaviour that you would like to work on in order to improve your management ability. When you close the book and are back in action you should be able to observe this new management behaviour in yourself. It's probably safe to say that the first few times will not satisfy you. That can be deflating.

I can imagine little Shirley Temple, the child star from the 1950s, singing her cute little number, "I pick myself up, wipe myself off, and start all over again." That's a good way of handling the failure. The more you stick with the desire to change and the harder you work at making the change, the better your chances.

What changes might you want to make as a result of reading this book? There could be several. From reading the first few chapters you might be surprised by how much better people listen to you when you are more empathetic. By developing the skill of genuinely listening to people and, if you will, speaking their language as you show them that you hear what they are saying, you can create a powerful rapport with those you lead.

When you learn from the chapter on vision what sort of things people are mumbling to themselves as they listen to you speak, you might want to adopt some of the speaking skills we consider there. You may also decide to change the way you describe what you want people to do, when you read about ways of dealing with employees who don't seem to take responsibility.

When you get to the chapter "Who Is Managing Whom?", you might recognize how your employees are pushing your buttons to get what they want. You may decide to be less vulnerable to their techniques.

Near the end of the book, we look at how to coach employees by balancing empathy and focus. You might be pleased to learn that there are effective ways to get people to change their behaviour. You may decide to work harder at finding the link between what you want from your people and what they want from their job. Trying to link their goals and your goals may be the most valuable shift in style you could ever make.

This is a key skill that arises throughout the book. It involves the ability to unite empathy and focus so that we see both sets of goals at once. This magical combination requires a practised effort to step outside our own self-limited view and into one that contains both our own and that of the people around us.

From this bird's-eye perspective, we can see what our employees seek and its relationship to what we seek, and formulate a mutually satisfying plan for goal fulfillment. This meta-level thinking, as I call it, is a great tool for communicating our concerns and ideas to employees. Our goal is to help them step outside themselves and see, from above, their own behaviours and attitudes. Then they can learn and grow. We bring value to people in this way.

Bringing value, I believe, is what our management role is all about. We reach our own goals by nurturing the people we lead or manage in a way that helps them reach *their* own goals. We aid our customers in this same way. When we stand back and look at the big picture, we can see the link between what our organization has to offer to customers, what our employees need in order to get where they want to be, and even what we can do for society with our own goals.

But meta-level thinking, accomplishing these grand objectives, requires a balanced focus on goals and attention to others, or empathy. It's a delicate balancing act.

It's also a generous gift, a gift of leadership. When you bring value to the people around you — your team members, your organization, your customers — you are making a very noble gesture. You become a conduit through which flows benefit for all. And you win in the process.

EMPATHY

ARE you usually an effective listener? No doubt you have good days and bad days. Sometimes we are highly self-oriented — too focused on our own thinking, our own goals, our own ego — and tend to connect with others a little less effectively. But on the whole, are you in the habit of stopping what you are doing and investing yourself in the person communicating with you? It's important — not just because you will understand what the person is saying but also because you will cause the person to feel heard. And a person who feels heard is much more likely to listen to you when it is your turn to speak.

Listening to our employees and letting them know that we understand their perspectives is a key to people management. But this doesn't just mean that we have to begin sentences with "I know what you mean, but . . ." In fact, most listeners probably feel frustration when they hear those words. The words send the message: shut up and listen.

If your employee says, "Why do I always have to sweep the floor?" or "I am reluctant to move on this acquisition because of the bad reputation it might give us," it would not make him feel particularly well respected if you responded, "I know what you mean, but you are going to do it anyway." Perhaps he would do what you asked him to do, but his private thoughts might be something like: "This person isn't listening and doesn't care about me."

What you could say instead is, "I know you sweep the floor all the time and it seems unfair, especially when it's such a drag to do, but it has to be done and I would really like you to do it." Or, if you don't like the long-winded approach, how about, "Yes, I know it's a drag — but please do it anyway." The goal is to make the person feel understood by capturing the essence of his opinion in your response. That's empathy.

The best definition I have seen for the word "empathy" involves the notion of identification. "I empathize with you" means "I can identify with you, I can see the world from your perspective, I can identify with the feelings you have about this!"

Empathy is not the same as sympathy. If someone grieves the loss of a loved one, and we are not doing any grieving over this loss ourselves, we sympathize with them. We are removed, standing on the sidelines. We care, perhaps, but we are not experiencing their feelings. We sympathize. That's not empathy. Effective communication with employees calls for more than sympathy. Empathy is a necessity.

On the other hand, our goal is not to fall prey to other people's sorrow either. We don't want to start weeping with everyone who laments in front of us. We would never get anything done. The position we seek is somewhere in the middle: between simply acknowledging the feelings of another person and being so empathetic that we lose track of ourselves.

THE LISTENING GAME

In 1952, the psychologist Dr. Carl Rogers wrote an article in the *Harvard Business Review* that told businesspeople how inadequately they communicate. Rogers wrote as a "client-centred therapist"; when people sought his therapeutic help, he let them do most of the talking. His job was to make people feel heard. We feel better, he said, when we know someone understands us. What we need is empathy from other people. Empathy is like a healing agent.

I learned by reading Carl Rogers of a listening game trainers play that provides first-hand experience of empathy. It's a somewhat scary or threatening game, but it can be very instructive. Consider trying it with someone you know well, maybe even an employee. I play it with my wife. Let me explain the game by describing a recent professional application.

I was asked to help a senior manager resolve a problem between two employees. One of the troubled people was a manager; let's call her Brenda. The other person was Brenda's subordinate, Christine. Brenda and Christine hated each other. In fact, their animosity was so profound that the senior manager said that if we couldn't fix this problem, Christine would be fired. (He believes in protecting his managers.) Brenda, Christine, and I went into a room alone and played the listening game.

My role was that of facilitator. And the rules are simple. One person says something to the other person, something honest and about the relationship, and lasting no more than thirty seconds. Then the other person paraphrases what was said, until the first person is satisfied that what she said was wholly heard. When that's done, it's time to switch roles, so both parties get to communicate what's on their minds.

I invited Brenda to go first. She said: "Christine, when you come to work in the morning you've got a scowl on your face and you don't say hello to people. It's unfriendly and it wrecks the morale on my team. And I don't like it."

Then I asked Christine to tell Brenda what she heard Brenda say, starting her sentence with the words "Brenda, I hear you saying . . ." So Christine started off: "Brenda, I hear you saying that you don't like me and you never did. You think people don't like me, and I think it's you they don't like."

Then, according to the rules, I turned to Brenda and asked, "Brenda, is that a 100 percent accurate depiction of what you tried to say — yes or no?" Brenda replied — no surprise here — "No." "Okay, Christine, try again."

Interestingly, Christine couldn't do it. So we got Brenda to repeat her statement. After a few tries, Christine finally satisfied Brenda that what Brenda said was wholly heard.

Then it was Christine's turn. She lamented the fact that Brenda talked to Christine's colleagues about her behind her back. Christine said she didn't trust Brenda and that nobody did, and that she just didn't like her. Well, poor communication skills are not just reserved for employees. Brenda also had to have the statement repeated. But ultimately, Christine got heard too.

The game went on like this for a few more rounds. It was a perfect example of how we don't listen. Our empathy skills, particularly when we are on the defensive, are not so hot. Rogers was right. But why? Why was it, for example, that neither Brenda nor Christine could hear a simple ten-second utterance from the other, such that each could repeat the gist of it? Imagine what a real conversation between these two is like.

I was reminded of an associate who once told me that he did some informal research on business conversations. He said that he approached twenty pairs of people after they had a normal business conversation and asked each member of the pair to recount the conclusions of their conversation. He reported that only one pair could both accurately describe what they concluded from their talk and capture all the nuances that were conveyed.

It's like we finish our conversations, both stand up, look each other squarely in the eyes, shake hands firmly, and in confident, professional voices declare, "Got it." But we did not get the message that the other person thinks was sent. We don't listen as well as we think.

Carl Rogers said, "Our tendency to evaluate intrudes on communication." We are usually so busy having private thoughts while we are listening — thinking about whether we like what we are hearing, or what we will say next, or what the consequences of what we are hearing might be, or that we have to pick up milk on the way home — that we just don't listen. (This "chattering" going on in our heads has also been called self-talk or explanatory style.)

And this assumes that what the person is saying is being said clearly. That's the other side of the coin. Matters get worse when we can't actually get clear thoughts out of our mouths: other people will have even less chance of getting our intended message. Nobody's getting anything right, and business goes on.

SILENT MUMBLING

Chatter is a problem. It's natural, but it intrudes. Go ahead, catch yourself doing it right now. The part of you that is doing the talking is referred to by some people as your ego, or your sense of "self." It is the source of defensiveness. It's the thing in other people that we have to allay. It's the thing in ourselves that we have to calm if we want to hear others clearly.

There is a certain paradox in these ideas: our self can be our own worst enemy. The more you want to get your way, the more the appetite to do so intrudes on getting it. This is because getting our own way with people depends on getting them to listen to us. When we strongly want our own way, we are likely to be less empathetic. When we are less empathetic, other people don't listen because their own chatter picks up speed. They are therefore less compliant, and we are left frustrated. So we want our way even more aggressively. Our aggressiveness shuts more people off. It's the proverbial vicious circle.

I see it as a consultant every day. I know of a senior vice-president who faces this problem. He has an unusually strong sense of self. That's what got him so far. He has always tended to get what he wanted. Very goal oriented, he's adept at the old push, push, push, press, press, press. He may be respected, but he is not liked. He projects no empathy. Of course, he is capable of having the same feelings that others have — he is human (though this claim might be challenged by some) — but his self-orientation is so strong that he is almost never in touch with how others feel. He is bright, so he understands people intellectually. But he doesn't feel their feelings, he doesn't identify with them.

He spends his days being frustrated by them. He wants to tell them what to do. He tries hard to make himself clear. But people don't get his messages because he doesn't empathize. Here's an excerpt from an actual conversation.

VP: How are things going with the new product
line? Are you on track with the schedule?
Director: Well, the accounting people haven't got the
billing system up yet so things are delayed
a bit.
VP: Why? I told you to go right to Bill. He's
the only guy with any brains over there.
Why didn't you just do what I said?
Director: Bill was away sick last week and then he had
to go to Chicago. He couldn't be reached.
So we dealt with Roger. He seemed to
understand what had to be done. He showed
us what was involved in getting the new
system going. It actually does look like a bit
of a monster. He asked for a couple of extra
weeks. It made sense, so I just changed the
schedule to make it all fit.
VP: (face beginning to contort with anger,
voice rising, everybody in the room bracing
themselves because the big guy is gonna
blow) I told you Bill was the only way to get
it done! You people aren't listening. I mean,
the whole budget depends on making this
work. The accounting people will never see
how this is supposed to go unless someone
tells them. The computer fields just need to
be adjusted so the database re-sorts. You

people need to get what I want. The problem
is not that the system needs to be fixed; MIS
can do the adjustment to the proximate.
Now, I want Mary to get the report from
MIS and arrange the whole thing.

Mary: (afraid to ask, afraid not to ask) I don't see
how MIS can adjust it until they get the
go-ahead from accounting.

VP: (now over the top) Just do it! It doesn't
matter what accounting says! The
marketplace isn't going to wait for a Chicago
flight to arrive. I don't think you people get
it. The friggin' thing is not that hard!
Doesn't the MIS report show the field?

Director: I don't think it works that way. Accounting
literally needs to reprogram from their end.

VP: (practically with tears in his eyes) Just do it!

By this time, the meeting was a lost cause. Nobody
would speak up because the big guy's sense of self, his
inexorable focus, wouldn't budge. There were legitimate
problems that he would hear nothing of. As a group,
the team could have sorted out a strategy, but things
stalled. Feelings were hurt. The project was slowed.
Everybody was upset for his or her own reasons.

After the meeting in which this exchange occurred,
the senior vice-president complained to me that people
don't listen. He asked, "Do we just have the wrong
people? They don't take responsibility. Every little
obstacle is a reason to lay down and die. I need people
who can get the job done."

In my opinion, this manager's high-focus/low-
empathy style is his downfall. His strength, his focus

on his goals, intrudes upon his ability to fulfill his goals. If he made people feel heard, they would relax and listen, and they would be able to create new ideas.

SELF-ORIENTATION/ OTHER-ORIENTATION

The senior VP's high goal-orientation shows up as "self-orientation" because he doesn't spend much time thinking of others. That is, he is usually thinking of himself and what he wants. Focus and self-orientation often go together in this way. Empathy and "other-orientation" are always related. It's as though our attention can be on only one thing at a time. A good day has us regularly shifting between being empathetic towards others and being focused on our goals.

You arrive at work in the morning and say hello to a colleague. The moment your attention is on your colleague, you are in an empathetic or other-oriented mode. After your greetings, it's back to self, as you think about your goals for the day. An employee approaches you. You chat for a few minutes. The following chart depicts how your empathy/focus might be expressed. Notice that you can still give bad news when you are empathetic.

Employee	What You Would Say If Empathetic	What You Would Say If Focused
I'm not sure how you want to handle the invoice for ABC.	What do you think?	Pay it.

Employee	What You Would Say If Empathetic	What You Would Say If Focused
Is there any way I can get my cheque early this pay day, since I'm going on vacation the day before pay day?	It would be nice to get the cheque before you go, so you don't have to scrounge around for money. Unfortunately, there's no way to adjust the system.	I'm afraid not. There's no way to adjust the system for early payment.
I'm afraid I lost my cool with this customer. He was obnoxious.	It's a drag to have rude people keep poking away like that — it can really push your buttons. But keep trying to see things their way.	You just can't keep losing it that way. We've talked about that before. You have to get control over this.

The distinction between self-orientation and other-orientation is a great way to understand how to make or break customer service as well. People are effective at service when they make customers feel heard. They are terrible when their empathy skills are weak. Examples abound. Not long ago I was on an aircraft next to a colleague. We were chatting about this exact distinction between self and other, and he wanted me to sketch a little diagram to explain the concept. I reached for my notebook and got a pen, but unfortunately, there were coffee cups between us. I looked for a flight attendant. Two of them were approaching us, one walking backwards, pulling a cart, her co-worker pushing the cart.

We awaited their arrival as they served nearby passengers. First the attendant with her back to us reached us. I said, "Would you mind removing these coffee cups, please? We'd like to make a little space." Her response, a perfect rendition of self-orientation, was, "Oh, we don't do that yet. This is the dessert service."

I looked at my friend. He smiled. "Who needs diagrams?" he said. We declined the cake and waited for opportunity number two. When the second flight attendant arrived, I made the same request, in the same tone. Her response? "Certainly, sir." She grabbed the cups, placed them on an empty shelf on the cart (to which the first attendant had easy access), and asked, "Would you care for dessert?"

The self/other distinction was clear. The first attendant's response to our request might be labelled "self." Coffee-cup removal was not on her agenda. Her brain was saying to itself, "I don't do that yet." The second attendant's thought was, "Somebody needs something." From a service perspective, we felt heard by the second. She was other-oriented.

Of course, how other-oriented you are varies. When you are being criticized, it may be more difficult to disengage from a defensive, self-oriented posture. When you are disappointed, you may become more focused than otherwise. When you are consciously focused on a goal, it is tougher to be more empathetic.

EMPATHY AND FOCUS

Empathy is an effort. For many of us, it is counter-intuitive. Living things tend towards survival. Plants turn their leaves to the sun to gather more light. Animals defend themselves for a living. Many of them wake up in the morning, defend themselves from being eaten by others, do things like kill others to stay alive, and then go to sleep to rest up so they can do it all again the next day. Many humans go through the same process. The notion of forgoing goal fulfillment in order to invest themselves in pure care for others does not come naturally. Thomas Hobbes said that, if left on their own, humans by nature would be at battle. Self-interest would rule. Empathy does not come naturally.

And empathy takes time. Sometimes when we just want what we want, we don't feel inclined to be thoughtful of others. We forget, perhaps, that attending to others can increase our chances of fulfilling our goals.

Can one be both empathetic and focused simultaneously? Yes. My experience is that, if we have effectively visualized our goals, and we understand them, we can afford to be more empathetic. We can authentically listen to people from what one might call foreground consciousness while sustaining our goal-orientation in background consciousness. If our goals are unclear, then any deliberate dedication to other people, any gesture of empathy, depletes our self-oriented focus.

If we do have goals nicely laid out in our minds, and we are engaged empathetically, then magic occurs. We can listen, respond caringly, and still lead the troops. Think of any good leader you admire. Doesn't that person's ability to simultaneously care about people and drive to their goals just shine?

It is work for most of us, however. Sometimes, it's an effort to care. We want what we want, and other people get in the way. It also takes time to express empathy. It's worth it, though — not for any moral reasons (though some could argue for them). Empathy, as we have seen, can be a tool.

What about you? If you surveyed those around you, would they give you a high score for listening, for projecting empathy? If they didn't find you empathetic, would they have the gumption to state their true feelings?

Do you have clear goals? Do you know where you are taking your team? Have you got a plan to get there? Do you start conversations and meetings with goals in mind or at least with an effort to define them? And if so, do you take the risk of relaxing them by dedicating yourself to the people in front of you?

It does feel like a risk to forfeit self in honour of other. After all, we might ask ourselves, what happens if we just wander off course? Doesn't being empathetic with someone mean taking his side? In the next chapter, we'll see how the answer to that question is no.

EMPATHY STOPS CHATTER

I N his 1995 book *Emotional Intelligence*, Harvard-trained psychologist Daniel Goleman tried to show that people who have a high level of "emotional intelligence" are far more likely to be successful than are people who have a low level. How high your IQ is doesn't predict how well you will relate to other people. Part of Goleman's definition of emotional intelligence was the ability to read other people. Getting along with others requires the ability to feel what they are feeling and to adjust yourself accordingly. Your employees need empathy in order to interact with customers, suppliers, the general public, and one another. As a manager, you need it too.

Are you in touch with your people? Can you feel the mood of a roomful of employees and capture that mood in your remarks? Equally important, can you be face-to-face with any one of your employees and feel what he or she is feeling? Can you do it when you are disappointed with the person? Or when the person disagrees with you? Empathy is much tougher when you are not in agreement. Are you effective at dealing with individuals when their opinions differ from your own?

In this chapter we will look at how to respond to

employees when there is tension between you. There is a two-step approach for handling those awkward moments. The first step involves empathy; it is when we cause the person to feel heard. The second step involves focus — offering your response, helping the person to see your point of view. The challenging part of the two-step dance is step one. When someone is pushing our buttons it is difficult to put that aside and listen. Doing so is counter-intuitive. But it's rational. It helps fulfill our goals. Let's take a look at the components of the two-step, one at a time.

EMPATHY

As managers we find ourselves in these situations frequently: assigning a task that we know the person won't like; offering criticism to someone who we predict will get defensive; dealing with someone we don't get along with; dealing with employee disputes; giving bad news, such as telling someone that they didn't get a promotion or that they've been laid off. Basically, using empathy is useful any time we are dealing with another person's ego or defensiveness.

People who don't get defensive are a treat to manage. You can be your focused, self-oriented self and they respond eagerly, compliantly. I work with someone like this. She never says "Yes, but . . . ," she does what she is asked to do, she gets along with others, she handles bad news well. Sometimes I feel guilty managing her. At raise time, I keep giving her lots of money.

It is when the other person is confrontational that management is more difficult — basically when his opinion conflicts with yours and he is stubborn about his opinion.

Of course, an employee's tendency to stand up for his rights, to speak her mind, to disagree is not a bad thing. Indeed, whole political systems are based on two poles in opposition. It's called a dialectic. It's healthy because two heads are better than one. It's the old thesis-antithesis-synthesis thing. Somebody has an opinion, a thesis. It leads to someone else taking the opposite side, the antithesis. They work things out, thereby reaching a synthesis. As managers we are interested in the synthesis component, reaching agreement. The use of empathy makes resolving tension easier, come faster, and feel better.

Let's consider a retail environment, although the number of possible situations is equal to the number of managers out there. A store manager named Joe wants an employee, Mike, to stay late to clean up. Joe knows that Mike won't want to do it — Mike stayed late last night and the night before. Joe could ask Linda, but she's engaged and has wedding things going on these days. She had previously arranged this night off. Mike is happy, more or less, for Linda, but he is getting a little tired of having to work extra hours.

Joe approaches Mike and says, "Mike, I'd like you to work late again tonight." Visibly upset, Mike says, "I can't tonight. I've made other plans. Sorry, boss." Joe says, "Well, there's nobody else. Linda's tied up — she arranged this night off months ago — and I've got to get to a meeting at head office, so, I'm sorry, but I need you to do it." Mike's voice gets a bit louder: "C'mon, Joe, this isn't fair. I've had to do a whole lot of extra stuff lately and I don't think I should have to do this. It's not like I'm paid a fortune, you've got me cleaning the top shelves because she's not tall enough, last night

I had those problems closing up and got home real late. I only got five hours' sleep. Give me a break!"

Here is Joe's big opportunity. He already showed a tiny amount of empathy when he said he was sorry, and he appealed to Mike's nice-guy side when he said he *needed* him to do it. If Joe was in a high-focus, low-empathy mode, he might now say, "Tough. This is retail, my friend. Welcome to the real world. You'll get your share of exceptions. But tonight, you're working late. Okay?" In this case, Joe has been firm. His chatter in his head might be, "Don't talk back to me, buddy. I'm in charge here." Mike's confrontational response has caused this manager to get defensive. His self-orientation is dominant. His goal of getting Mike to work late has stayed in focus. But his empathy projection, his other-orientation, is low.

But, you might ask, what's so wrong with Joe's approach? Life is like this, right? Sometimes managers have to be firm.

Maybe. Even if Mike does stay late tonight, my bet is that he resents it. Tomorrow will probably see extra tension in the store. Perhaps the extra tension will go away. But if Joe's style doesn't change, I believe he may ultimately deplete the energy level of his employees. They may feel less empowered and their self-esteem could slowly decline. Also the store's financial performance could be affected. Twelve months of this style of management can make a store perform at less than its potential. When people go looking for the answer to poor performance, they might never find it.

Let's look at a slightly more balanced, more empathetic approach that Joe might take. "Mike, I know you feel there's an imbalance here, and you're right. You've been doing more than your share of the cleaning, just because Linda's shorter than you. And last night's staying late was a favour. And having to stay extra-late because of the door was a real drag. So my asking you to stay late all over again has to feel like you are being taken advantage of. But we're in a jam here. Linda asked for this day off a long time ago. I do have to go downtown at closing time. I can't think of another way to handle it. Yes, it's a real drag. It's got to be done. Okay?"

In this case, Joe has tried to capture the essence of Mike's feelings. The more accurate the depiction of Mike's perspective, the more powerful the empathy gesture will be. He has taken essentially the same stubborn position, but it probably will have fewer negative consequences. Mike will feel heard. The empathy has a certain ameliorating effect. Reality is still the same — Mike has to work late — but steps have been taken to reduce the resentment.

Of course, if Joe really wanted to reduce the resentment, he would work out a deal. Maybe Mike can take off now for a few hours in exchange for having to work tonight. Maybe Joe can explain to Linda the way Mike feels and she can agree to do something extra for him. There are many possibilities. The point is that Joe's high-focus response had the effect of shutting things down. He got what he wanted in the short term, perhaps, but he still shut things down. The more other-oriented response leads to a better resolution.

Did Joe's empathy gesture look artificial to you? Was it a con job? My opinion is that it's only slippery if it's done with slippery intentions. That is, if Joe's self-talk is "I can schmooze this guy and get what I want, then this will be done," then Joe may not sleep so well at night. On the other hand, if Joe is truly listening to Mike, honestly getting in touch with how his employee feels, then Joe is being straight.

Notice the two parts to Joe's more empathetic approach. Before the tension arose, Joe stated his goal. Then came the tension. In response to Mike, Joe first showed empathy, he showed he understood how Mike felt. After that he restated his goal. Press and release. This pattern will recur throughout this book. If it's always press, press, press, then nobody likes you. If it's always release, release, release, then you are not really leading people at all. If you both press *and* release, you achieve balance in your communication.

There are various ways of projecting empathy. Sometimes we can just make an emotional, compassionate sound: "Yeah, I know." At other times, we expand on the other person's point — briefly, perhaps, but we must make them feel understood, we must make it clear that their feelings are validated. For example, let's assume you want to say to me right now, "This point about empathy is self-evident. I do it all the time." Here are some high-focus/low-empathy responses.

- No, it's not.
- I know, I know. Hang on, though. It's when you are getting defensive that this stuff is more valuable.
- Why do you say that? Have we got a bit of an attitude problem here?

Here are some other-oriented, low-focus responses.

- Oh. I guess you should stop reading, then.
- Sorry. I hope the next part is more satisfying for you.
- Hari-kiri seems appropriate here, I guess. Please pass the knife.

Here are some balanced responses.

- I know what you mean, it does seem simplistic, doesn't it? When our ego is not engaged, empathy can flow quite easily. It's when we get defensive that things are tougher.
- Yes. While reading this, the method we are looking at does look trite, doesn't it? On the other hand, your ego is probably not engaged yet. Think of what you would be like if you were in an argument.
- Yes, simplistic, huh? Especially when you're reading a book to get value and you find your time being wasted. It's interesting, though, it's when your ego is engaged that this stuff comes alive. You see . . .

One of the difficult parts of demonstrating empathy is staying brief. We need to avoid getting long-winded. There are many reasons for this, not the least of which is that we might lose track of our goals if we spend too much time running with the other person's perspective. Another reason for brevity is that we don't want to bore our listeners.

But perhaps the most difficult part of demonstrating empathy is in *finding* the empathy. The listening game described in the previous chapter shows participants how hard it is to listen. Christine and Brenda had their proverbial backs up when they tried to listen to each other; listening in that situation is very difficult. It's usually easy to empathize when we agree with someone or when we are relaxed and perhaps uninvolved in the feelings with which we want to identify. But when we are on the defensive, it's tough.

The next time you have a spat with someone, perhaps a loved one, try to play the game. You will probably discover that the more provocative the other person's comments are, the harder it is for you to accurately repeat what was said. I've watched some very bright people suddenly go empty-headed when they are trying to express empathy with someone who is criticizing them.

If I say to you that I don't like the way you are reading this book, how you are not paying enough attention to the details, then you may be able to paraphrase my message to you. However, if I then link my criticism to what perhaps is your habitual laziness when it comes to learning new ideas and how the fact that you have not been promoted as far up the ladder as you have wanted in your career probably stems from the same intellectual weakness, listening gets a little tougher for you — things are a little too close to home. If you also perceive that there may be a grain of truth in my claim, it gets tougher still. And if I actually knew you, and you held my opinion in some esteem, you might be surprised at how your brain shuts down when you try to empathize. Ego intrudes.

Think of when you speak with your employees. Many of them hang on your every word. Your glib comments can send them into a tailspin. Your criticisms, comments that may seem minor to you, are very easily misunderstood.

But empathy stops chatter. If you empathize with your people, they will be able to relax. If you simply press, press, press, then they will get defensive and not hear you. But here comes the paradox again. Their not hearing you triggers more aggressive behaviour on your part. This in turn causes their hearing skills to dwindle even more. The way out of this downward spiral is for you to be empathetic as a communicator.

Probably the simplest way to develop the skill is to envision your listener's self-talk and run with it. That is, put yourself in her shoes, hearing what you are saying, and think of what is going through her mind. Say out loud, speculatively, tentatively, what you think she might be feeling, and check her response. If you seem to be on track, go further with it, even though it might feel risky. Fuel her perspective.

The worst-case scenario is that you will rethink your position. That can't be so bad — after all, it is your position and you're doing the rethinking. The best-case scenario, the one that surprisingly is most likely to occur, is that the other person will feel touched by you. She will feel heard and understood. Then she will relax, and be open to your input.

So the first step in responding to negativity is to empathize. The second step is easier. You get to tell the other person your way of seeing the world.

FOCUS

The kinds of things we say after empathizing fall into four categories. We say the equivalent of "Tough — that's the way it is," or "Okay, here's what we'll do," or "For this, I apologize. There are no excuses," or, finally, "It's actually good news." Each one represents an option for step two of the two-step.

"TOUGH — THAT'S THE WAY IT IS"

The "Tough" response is what you use when no change is available. You can't or won't budge. If somebody wants a promotion and you are giving it to someone else, you would use this response.

Of course, you don't just say "Tough." All four responses call for an initial gesture of empathy. In this case, after advising a person that he did not get a promotion, you might say, "Bob, the truth of the matter is that you could do this job — you've got the experience and the knowledge. Let's face it, we both know that you've shown lots of dedication. And I know that you really want it. The fact is that Mary has been offered the position and she has accepted it. I want you to find a way to accept this news, Bob. I'd like you to support her in her new role. And I'd like you to do so with a positive attitude. Please don't underestimate my respect for you."

Press and release. In this case, delivering the bad news represents your pressing your will. Release is communicated in the empathy you show to Bob. Press is when you make it clear that Mary won the position and how you want Bob to respond. Release is revisited when you remind him of your respect for him.

Financial issues, employment matters, and decisions you have made that have to be accepted are situations that call for the "Tough" response. It could easily be seen as the most difficult step-two option to employ, not just because it involves giving bad news but also because it is as far from the step-one empathy gesture as one can get.

"OKAY, HERE'S WHAT WE'LL DO"

Ideally, this is the most often used response after your empathy gesture. It often follows a dialectic: the other person wants or thinks x, you want or think y, you compromise with a change in plan that suits your needs.

In the case of Joe and Mike, Joe agreeing with Mike to negotiate with Linda is an example of his employing the "Okay, Here's What We'll Do" response.

"FOR THIS, I APOLOGIZE. THERE ARE NO EXCUSES"

This response is appropriate when excuses or explanations just sound defensive. If you promised someone you would do his review and you broke the promise, only to repromise and renege yet again, then the appropriate response is a straightforward apology. It is not something you do if you propose some solution or promise some other next step; doing that would be the "Okay, Here's What We'll Do" response.

When you have screwed up royally, then you just apologize. Last week I promised to call a bank for an employee. I failed to fulfill the promise. The employee had a bit of a hassle because of my neglect. I had to empathize and apologize. I said, "Ah, Todd, that's got

to drive you crazy. I really let you down. It's unaccept-
able. I apologize — no excuses. Sorry." It was too late
to call the bank or help him in some other way. The
apology was all I could offer.

"IT'S ACTUALLY GOOD NEWS"

This response is one you use when an employee is
missing a point or an opportunity. For example, if
someone is upset because one of his colleagues didn't
do a report on time, but you know that by not doing
the report your team will be able to take advantage of
slightly higher performance statistics, you could say,
"Yeah, it's frustrating when you expect the data on your
desk and once again it's not there. In this case, it's actually good news, though, because I told him to hold off
in order to include the XYZ sale. It's going to affect all
of our bonuses."

Here's another game to play. Let someone be negative about you, for fun. (Try a friend or loved one —
it's a safer experiment that way.) Tell them you are
going to give four different responses to the criticism.
Start by soliciting the negativity. Then use empathy
and one of the four responses. Get the person to state
the criticism yet again; then you empathize and
respond once more, only this time with a different one
of the four responses.

Let's say your spouse chooses to complain about
your not cleaning up a certain mess, as you had
promised. Here are the four possible responses. Notice
the empathy employed prior to each.

"Tough — that's the way it is"	I know it drives you crazy when I don't do what I say. It's like you can't count on me. And I know you hate living with a mess. But sometimes, I just get wrapped up. I'm not going to pretend it's not going to happen.
"Okay, here's what we'll do"	Yeah, that's got to drive you crazy. I'll do it right now.
"For this, I apologize. There are no excuses"	And you hate messes too. And broken promises. You know what? I apologize. I humbly apologize.
"It's actually good news"	I know. The place is a mess. And I broke a promise. And that's offensive. Good news, though: instead of doing that, I went out and got you this brand-new dream home.

TROUBLE WITH THE TWO-STEP

When teaching managers the two-step model for dealing with upset employees, certain patterns show up. One mentioned above is that people tend to find the "Tough" response the most difficult. My experience, though, is that the higher one climbs in one's career, the more frequently the "Tough" response has to be used. For this reason, it's worth practising.

Another pattern is that managers think they are empathizing when in fact they are not. The importance of this point should not be underestimated. Let me give you an example from my own life. My son and I went into a hamburger joint — one that prides itself on its service. My son went to the counter to place our order and I grabbed a booth. This place sells two kinds of fries, curly and straight — curly is the costly one. My son asked for one of their combination plates but he wanted to substitute curly fries for straight fries. The service person thought he obviously was from another planet. She condescendingly pointed out that there were no substitutions, period.

Son turns to father and calls for help from the big guy by using a stunned-looking eyebrow raise. I sidle up to the bar and the manager steps in. Presumably he has overheard everything so far. So I make the same request. He says, "No, sorry, no substitutions." He probably thought that the "sorry" part was the empathy mission fulfilled.

So I tried some empathy. "Well, how about you just give him the combo with a half order of curly fries and I'm sure we'll all be happy — he gets the fries, you probably save money since the curlies can't cost you double the straights, and everybody's happy." He says, "I'm sure it's frustrating, sir, but there are no substitutions. If we did it for you, we'd have to do it for everybody."

Clearly our friend was using the two-step. His step-two selection was "Tough — that's the way it is." He probably would suggest that the "I'm sure it's frustrating" offering was empathy. But was it?

Not a chance. I had proposed a deal. His mission was to make me feel heard. For example, he could have said, "That does sound like a neat deal, sir — it looks like a mutual win, and it's simple. Unfortunately . . ." But he didn't make me feel heard. And as soon as I sensed that he wasn't capturing my last point, the chatter in my head picked up speed. His effort at empathy was not good enough. We left.

Still another pattern in the use of this model is long-windedness. Showing empathy for too long sounds artificial — unctuous is the best word for it. And it's a bad thing. The ethics of this process is similar to the ethics of selling. Just as a salesperson may be unethical when she lies or feigns sincerity, so too are the rest of us when we don't mean what we are saying.

But you may wonder how you can empathize with someone when you just don't agree with his perspective. Remember, though, that this process is not about agreeing with people so that you can win them over. Instead, it is about seeing their point of view so that you can communicate in a two-way context. It shows respect for other people.

If you say clearly that Percival is a liar and I believe he is not, I won't empathize with you by saying that yes, Percival is a liar. That would be dishonest of me. Indeed, in order for me to empathize with your perspective, I may ask you why you feel that way. Or I may say, "If Percival is a liar, then I can understand why you would want to steer clear of him. My point, however, is that I don't think he is a liar, and that is why I am taking my position about him." In other words, I am recognizing the principle you are calling upon — that liars should not be trusted.

The goal in all of this is to validate the other's point of view. We want to pay respect to their right to their own opinion. When we show this respect, the other person will be inclined to offer the same to us. And we have an improved chance of fulfilling our goals.

DIFFERENT STROKES FOR DIFFERENT FOLKS

AS a manager your job often is to win people over to a desired point of view. Empathy plays a key part in accomplishing this. We have seen that if we are in touch with the points of view of others we are able to make them open to new perspectives. Empathy is a tool for making a person feel heard. It is an other-oriented gesture that creates a sense of commonality between you and the other person.

There are other ways to build this commonality aside from making people feel listened to. You can cause them to feel generally better understood. As a result, they feel you are speaking their language, that you share a way of thinking or a set of values. It starts with your being able to recognize their style. Adopting another's style of thinking results in a closer alignment with that person.

For centuries people have been categorizing styles of thinking. In a sense, it's a process of pigeon-holing people. "Bill has a temper when things get stressful, while Rob is very calm under pressure." "Linda is very logical and Mary leans more towards the creative." We quite naturally tend to make observations of the people around us and categorize them. It's almost a result of human language. Any time we can ascribe a character-istic to something — we might use an adjective or adverb to describe it — we have a different or opposite trait to which we can compare it. On or off, big or small, true or false, happy or sad, good or bad. If we have an *x*, we can conceive of *not x*. You might say it's the way our brains handle reality.

CLASSIFYING PEOPLE

All this is to say that we have been making observa-tions about our fellow human beings for a long time. Many polarities exist that explain how we behave. A polarity drives the message of this book, of course: balancing your quest to fulfill your own and your com-pany's goals with empathy for other people — self and other. This is one way that we can classify people. Although most of us are usually self-oriented when we are alone and awake, while interacting with other peo-ple, we may be other-oriented at one moment and self-oriented at another. If we add up a long series of moments with other people, we would find that most of us would more often fall into one category than the other. Generally, when we refer to someone as being "self-oriented," we are referring to when they are with other people and we are saying that they tend not to be very empathetic.

It gets interesting when you recognize that it is eas-ier to create commonality with people when you know which way they lean over time. Self-oriented people, for example, tend to be somewhat egocentric, while other-oriented people are more empathetic. If you reach the conclusion that someone is self-oriented, you personally derive some benefit. You know intuitively that if you provide the person with recognition, you give her pleasure and in doing so reduce her chatter. If her self-talk is frequently muttering "What about me? What about me?", you are able to slow down that self-talk when you can talk about her. Empathy stops chatter.

Spending a moment thinking about another's self-orientation will also help you realize what problems might ensue from that trait. If the self-oriented person works with other highly self-oriented individuals, a competitive atmosphere may pervade the office. You, as the manager, may have to speak to the person about the effects of his self-orientation. How to do that will be considered in chapter 5, when we talk about troublesome patterns in people's self-talk, as well as in chapter 9, when we look at how to handle a coaching conversation.

For now we are discussing personality types, a topic that has been well researched and is covered in many management training programs. By listing a series of dimensions, or polarities, and considering a person against each of them, you can build a profile of the person that, among other things, allows you to predict how that person will behave in a certain circumstance. The profile is essentially a personality analysis.

One model, referred to by some as the theory of social styles, considers two dimensions: assertiveness and task-orientation. By this theory, somebody might be very assertive and task oriented. Another person might be just as assertive and not very task oriented. There are four permutations or "types" of people, who, according to the model, are labelled "amiable" (low assertive, low task); "expressive" (high assertive, low task); "analytical" (low assertive, high task) and "driver" (high assertive, high task).

Another model uses four dimensions. Developed by Isabel Myers and Katharine Briggs in the 1940s, the model considers how we source our energy, how we take in information, how we make decisions, and how we organize our life. Each of these four dimensions has two poles: extroverted or introverted; sensing or intuition; thinking or feeling; and judgment or perception, respectively. In this model there are sixteen possible types of people.

Other models employ these and other traits for consideration. For example, intelligence, speed of thought, divergent versus convergent learning styles, perceptual dominance (auditory, visual, kinesthetic, and gustatory), internal versus external — the list of ways to categorize people is huge, probably equal to the number of adjectives that describe people on the job.

A MODEL FOR MANAGERS

For our purposes here, certain dimensions or human traits are particularly useful to think about. By analysing these dimensions we will create our own model. It is a simple one. The dimensions it considers are easily understood and recognized in others. They represent ways for you to modify your communication style in order to optimize the support of the people you work with.

The dimensions in our model are self- versus other-oriented (the polarity central to this book); feeling versus thinking (decision style); proactive versus reactive; and extroverted versus introverted. Each of these dimensions comes in degrees. We are not likely to be at one end of the scale or at the other. We tend to fall somewhere between the two extremes within each dimension.

Our behaviour varies as well. For example, we may be mildly self-oriented when we are with other people, but not all the time we are with other people. However, we tend to exhibit trends. In this book we are interested in the trends so that as managers we are able to build commonality with our employees. When someone is behaving in a self-oriented manner, we will know that to get the person to listen, we have to speak to him in a way that brings attention to him.

SELF-ORIENTED VERSUS OTHER-ORIENTED

Very rarely do we come across people who are always self-oriented in the company of others. Most of us spend varying amounts of time being in a self-oriented mode. When we are being self-oriented, we are, by definition, not being empathetic. To say that a person is very self-oriented means that the person is usually preoccupied with himself, even in the company of others. Kids are usually self-oriented. Their concerns are not usually for other people. As soon as they recognize that they are unique individuals, they want what they want. By the time they raise their own kids, they have the ability to be other-oriented. Infants don't do as well being taken care of by a non-empathetic parent.

When our survival is in question, we tend to be more self-oriented. It's a natural reaction to a threat. If you manage a team of people who are worried about their jobs, they likely will not tend to customers effectively. Nor will they listen very well to you, or anyone else. You can't be empathetic and self-oriented at the same time, unless you have managed to get into a linkage-based zone (which we shall look at in chapter 8).

Self-oriented people, particularly when they are somewhat extroverted, tend to like attention. You find them talking about themselves quite readily, and they use the word "I" more often than those who tend to be other-oriented. Conversations usually revolve around them.

To build rapport with people of this type, it is, predictably, useful to talk about them. They will be eager to hear of your plans for them and what they can do to go where they want. For example, instead of saying something like "Jeff, please form a little task force and develop a plan to address this problem," you might word your request like this: "Jeff, I'm confident that you've got some valuable perspectives on this matter. And I want to hear them. I also want other people to be actively involved in finding a solution. So I'd like you to head up a team to figure out a solution. Be careful you don't dominate the team, though. We need everybody to feel that they contributed. Try your best to encourage involvement. You can do it."

For you to deal effectively with a self-oriented person, you'll have to go into an other-oriented mode yourself. And if you naturally tend to be self-oriented, you will probably be challenged by managing a self-oriented person. Be careful that your own egocentric need for recognition does not cloud your ability to manage people similar to yourself.

Extroverted self-oriented people have traditionally

been effective in sales roles. They tend to have high "ego drive," meaning that they derive their satisfaction from influencing others. However, as customers move more and more towards wanting to buy from people who offer genuine expertise and who have the customers' best interests at heart, it is quite possible that other-oriented salespeople employing authentic consultative selling skills will make up the sales teams of the future.

Other-oriented people are great in service roles. Their instant response to people is to be empathetic, and they tend to listen well. They may not have the comparative focus of self-oriented people, however. This is because self-oriented people want what they want when they want it, and, as a result, tend to be very focused in their effort to get it. However, this does not mean that other-oriented people cannot be highly focused (think of Mother Teresa).

A person might be self-oriented at work and other-oriented at home. The reverse can also be true. The key is that when you want to get someone who is in an other-oriented mode to listen to you, it is prudent to talk about the people they care about. If an employee is saying, "We're not satisfying our customers by having this minimum-order policy," don't respond by saying, "They have no choice, we'll go broke if we deliver one peanut at a time." Instead say, "Yes, and we can't afford to upset our customers. We have to think of a way to make this habit of taking small orders work. We have a difficult situation here. What do you think we should do?"

FEELING VERSUS THINKING (DECISION STYLE)

Feeling-oriented people make decisions based on how they feel or what they personally value. A feeling-oriented person may choose a car because of its colour. A thinking-oriented person may base her choice on the vehicle's mileage or repair record.

If you are attempting to get feeling people onside with your point of view as a manager, it is important to appeal to their feelings. It is valuable to know what these people feel strongly about and link that to your message. If they are feeling it is unfair to overwork them the way you allegedly have been doing, don't cite statistics or the law or your rights. Instead, after showing some empathy for their position (something we attempt to do with all people since we are effective managers), try talking with them about the mission or the value they are bringing to those they care about.

On the other hand, if you are talking to a group of logicians — thinking types — about their work load, then you can dabble in statistics or history or the facts about the correlation between hard work and personal satisfaction. That's how thinkers work things through for themselves: they gather data and make a logical analysis. Logic works on thinkers, whereas an appeal to emotions — which are the results of value judgments — pulls the strings of the feeling types.

If you are a feeling type and you are talking to a thinking type, or vice versa, you probably should plan on doing what you are not comfortable doing — adopting a different style. (That's why they call it work, right?) Unfortunately, to win people over to our point of view, we usually can't just be ourselves. It's a press and release situation. It calls for interpersonal versatility. Effectively getting along with other people calls for effort.

It would be incorrect to assume that other-oriented and feeling types are the same thing, or that self-oriented people tend to be logical. Indeed, there are many people who are self-oriented and feeling-oriented at the same time. It is equally easy to find someone who is other-oriented and logical in approach.

PROACTIVE VERSUS REACTIVE

Proactive people tend to make lists and get things done before it's too late. They anticipate problems and solve them in advance. They build systems for themselves and others in order to avoid problems down the road. Managing proactive types is fairly easy. Give them a goal, state the schedule, provide the resources, and let them go.

Reactive types, on the other hand, tend to busy themselves with the present. They are often procrastinators. They may get things done, but they tend to do so at the last minute. They can be very frustrating to manage. If you manage reactive types, setting deadlines are crucial. It is even prudent to build hedges into deadlines you assign, in order to account for unexpected glitches. It is also helpful, when you assign tasks, to give these people something to react to. Typically, reactive types either need life to be made easy for them or they need some form of threat to compensate for their lack of self-motivation. You might, for example, give them a job to do by saying, "Bob, I need this report to be done on time or it's going to slow the whole office down, and everybody will be frustrated with us, okay?"

On the other hand, if Rick were a proactive person, you would entice him with a positive goal: "Rick, by getting this report done by the due date, we'll make friends all over the place, okay?" Notice how Bob gets the same essential message that Rick gets. It's just that you frame your delivery to match the way the different recipients like to receive requests.

It is unfortunate that we have to point out consequences to reactive types. But it is the way their brains deal with life. If they confront an obstacle, they tend to avoid it. So if you confront them with some predicted misfortune, they will avoid it as well. It's almost as though you have to trick them.

Proactive types hate such trickery. They tend to be repulsed by a manager who warns of negative consequences. If you are a reactive type who thinks in terms of avoiding negative consequences, and you are prone to making the feared negative consequences nice and clear to proactive people, then you are creating a negative environment that they will dislike.

If you are a reactive type and you manage proactive people, then you are probably creating all sorts of other frustration around you too. Your people probably feel that you sit on too many matters and they have to wait too long for answers. The best advice I've heard for reactive managers who lead a team of proactives is to delegate thoroughly. Make it so that you are not part of the process.

And if you have to be part of the process, then make it so that the process is defined in chunks — pre-you and post-you. For example, if in order to get a report completed you need to see a first draft from one person so that you can edit it and give it to another person to do touch-ups, then define the job for the first person as one of simply creating the first draft. Don't position it like the person is part of a process; make her task complete in itself. In this way she is accountable for a portion of it rather than the whole project, and no longer has to fret about it.

EXTROVERTED VERSUS INTROVERTED

Introverts tend to have a lot of things going on inside their minds, so additional stimulus from outside is undesirable. Extroverts, on the other hand, crave additional stimulus to bring them up to a satisfying level. It's like each of us has a certain noise comfort setting. We seek outside noise to reach the desired level — unless we have already reached it internally, in which case we seek to shield ourselves from the outside noise. Extroverts are statistically more likely to enjoy biting into a raw lemon and they are more likely to enjoy crunchy peanut butter. They like external stimulation because it makes them feel comfortable.

As a manager you need to check in with introverts fairly regularly. If something is bothering them, they are not naturally inclined to discuss it with you. It can bug them until they surprise you with their resignation. Often people leave jobs for reasons that could have been addressed if only an environment of open communication had been created.

It is smart to organize work areas where extroverts are with extroverts and introverts are with introverts. Mixing the two tends to lead to unhappy teams. I can think of an office environment where a virtual employment crisis occurred when a manager installed an extrovert "to liven up the team." The manager initially had a group of employees who were conscientious yet quiet. The manager misinterpreted the low amount of noise as bad morale: seven people spent day after day with little talk amongst themselves and little apparent fun in the office. He was concerned. So when he hired a new person to join the team, he deliberately brought on a dynamo. The individual was gregarious, liked to make fun, needed to have music in the background, and would make a great social convener for the team. After two months, the introverts approached the manager with concerns about how the new fellow was just not fitting in. The manager recognized that he had misdiagnosed a problem and corrected it by offering the extrovert a position elsewhere in the company.

If you are an extrovert, you probably come on too strong for the introverts around you. Compensate by employing your other-orientation to lower the volume of your voice and to slow down the speed of your speech.

If you are an introvert, then, although you may not enjoy the company of the extroverts around you, it is smart to acknowledge that they play a key role in your organization. Some of your customers may be extroverts who find introverts as unattractive to deal with as you might find those loud people around you.

Often managers hire mirrors. People tend to like themselves. After all, who could employ our unconscious value system better than we do ourselves? People are drawn to others who are like them or whom they wish they were like. For example, if you are an other-oriented introvert who is a thinking type and who is proactive — let's say, an accountant — and you are interviewing candidates, you will very likely find yourself drawn to effective listeners who are quiet, logical, and proactive.

As a consultant I have frequently marvelled at how many offices are staffed by people who are just like the boss. And I have also often noted that when a manager moves on, her replacement comes in, sees the old team, and says, "No, we've got all the wrong people — I can fix this place."

Yet at the same time, it is good to have a mixed bag of employees, not only because we want to optimize our versatility with customers but also because each trait has its advantages. Homogeneity is secure and non-threatening but it detracts from creativity, from the tension between differences that leads to healthy, evolving systems and ideas, and from the different perspectives that various types of people have to offer.

For example, extroverts can make friends with a range of customers. They will speak up when things go wrong and advise you of ways to make change that you may never hear from an introvert. Introverts bring concentration and the ability to appeal to other quiet types. They can also make a fine audience for the extroverts they interact with.

To be effective managers, then, we must modify our style in order to stop the chatter of our employees. We need the ability to shift into an other-oriented mode. People won't see our point of view unless we empathize and unless we "speak their language."

By developing our ability to build commonality we are able to lead. That's what effective managers do — they present a vision of the future and they lead people to it.

VISION FOUR

I N the 1990s corporations spent a lot of time sorting out values, strategies, vision statements, mission statements, objectives, and other tools designed to define directions and goals. The time and effort spent on these endeavours was, I believe, intended to satisfy a human need for knowledge of where we're going and how we are going to get there.

I sometimes think those efforts were compensating for a certain weakness amongst leaders. The leaders didn't know where to go or how to get there, so they involved the troops in developing answers for them. At the same time, I believe firmly that involving employees in developing values, visions, missions, objectives, and strategies goes a long way towards improved clarity and support of the conclusions.

People use the terms above in a whole lot of different ways. For me, *values* are things we believe in or think are important, such as honesty and profits. A *mission* is a description of what we are doing for a living; it is about the present, not the future, and it usually follows from a set of values put into a context (like the hardware business or the hardware distribution context). A *vision* is a detailed picture of how things will look if we have done a certain thing well. Sometimes it's a big picture; sometimes it's small. A *strategy* is a plan. In this chapter I will focus on vision.

One of the keys to being a good manager is helping your employees own, and be reminded of, a sense of vision. Without it, your team will likely wander off track. With a clear vision they will stay on track.

Vision is an interesting term when thought about in the context of self-talk or chatter. The leader's job is to be intimately involved in developing a vision, communicating it, and reminding people of it. A team's vision can become a predominant part of its members' self-talk. The team's vision makes for better self-talk than a team member's private, sometimes negative chatter.

A good leader encourages the troops to help create and develop goals and plans. How much involvement the leader has depends on a lot of factors: the maturity of the people being led, the sophistication of the leader, the nature of the industry and its products, and recent events. I don't believe that in business either autocracy or democracy work particularly well. Something in the middle seems healthy. Press and release. The leader's job is to keep people on track.

SUPPLYING THE SELF-TALK

Here's a claim for you: If you don't show your people how to see the world, you are leaving it up to them, and their view probably won't satisfy you. The job of the manager, at whatever level, is to supply the self-talk. If you don't supply the self-talk, the people who work for you will supply their own; you will be letting all the life experiences of your people, all the bad parenting, all the negative cliques in the work-place, all the neuroses built over tough lifetimes, run your team. This is a problem.

It is said that if you put somebody alone in a room for long enough, they'll get depressed. Eventually their self-talk turns to the negative. Apparently bachelors are most depressed on Sunday afternoons. They have had their weekend of fun, things wind down, idle time arrives, negativity sets in. The same applies to vacation time. Near the end, when boredom sets in, many people begin to feel depressed. "An idle mind is the devil's playground." Some people fill idle minds with religion. Good managers, knowing that without input people wander astray, provide a clear vision of the future, of how their teams will work towards a defined goal.

The rule being played with here also applies to raising kids. If you don't tell your kids how to see the world, you leave it up to them, and chances are their view won't please you. Indeed, kids need input. They need boundaries to learn how to survive. You could say that the job of parenting is to prepare kids for survival and happiness in adulthood. Parents have some model in their heads for how to succeed in the world. They want to give the model to their children. The model becomes the goal. The job of parents is to keep their kids on track.

A significant phase in child development occurs when kids figure out that Mommy and Daddy don't know what they are doing. "You mean grownups cry too?" "Grownups get scared?" Kids want to know that their parents have a plan. They get insecure when they discover otherwise. As adults, we are similar. We need to know that our bosses have a plan.

I've left my share of boardrooms where senior folks are struggling with indecision, poorly defined goals — or worse, no goals — and an insecurity that comes from not knowing what is going to happen or what they are going to do. I have closed the door behind me and listened to frontline troops express frustration because senior management isn't telling them some master plan, as though the plan was being kept secret. I've frequently found myself torn between, on the one hand, wanting to say "Don't worry, they don't know what they are doing either" and, on the other hand, trying to give a sense of security by reminding people that this is the information age, constant change is part of the gig, "embrace the ambiguity." But employees need input, even if it's intangible or tentative. At the very least they need to see that Mommy and Daddy have a plan to make a plan.

POINTING THE WAY

If I drive a bus full of people out to a field and invite them off the bus, they'll stand around waiting for instructions. If I then yell "Go!" they'll laugh a bit and with enough time just wander around or sit idly, like, if you will, cattle grazing the planet. If I then point out a tower off in the distance, they'll walk towards it. They won't walk straight to the tower: it will be a bit of a zig-zag route, since they'll be talking to one another and wandering off course a tad. They would have to focus on the tower to make it a straight line.

This leads me to two simple guidelines. First, the more often you glance at the goal, the straighter the path. Second, the better visualized the goal, the greater the focus. The job of managers, I propose, is to help people visualize the goal, and when they wander off track, as people are wont to do, to help them get back on track. You set the goal and send them on their way. You remind them of the goal, and set them free once again. Press and release.

This principle applies as well to people involved in promoting products. If you don't tell your marketplace — your customers — how to see your company and its products, then you are leaving it up to the competition, whose view of your company is unlikely to please you.

It even applies to self-management. If you don't tell yourself how to see the world, then you leave it up to various unguided programs in your head. Prisoners of war replaced negative self-talk with concentration on a defined topic. In his book *Man's Search for Meaning*, Victor Frankel describes how prisoners of war during the Holocaust were more likely to survive if they held on to hope. Those who stopped hoping spiralled down to greater and greater depths of ill health and despair.

Meditation and mind control can involve ridding oneself, in one way or another, of stray and random thoughts and focusing on one single thought. We have lots of self-talk going on in our heads. We can let it roll randomly, and thereby maybe get negative, or we can be responsible for what's going on in there. We can be focused.

That's the job of managers. We are agents. We have will. We choose where we want to go and we focus on it. We're driving the bus. We're nice about it, empathetic, that is: we help people get on the bus with a smile on our face, we drive thoughtfully, carefully, we make conversation along the way. But we're definitely driving the bus.

The description of the destination and the means to the destination make up what I refer to as vision. First of all, it's a visual thing, meant to be seen by the mind's eye. It's also about the future: it's the place we want to get to. It's worth getting to — it's better than the present. It's connected to the customer, usually, since that is what we're all about. With luck, it's vivid for all — that is, clearly outlined.

Vision does not have to be a big-picture thing, like our role in society or our operating principles. It can be as simple as the following, for someone who's on the job for the first day: "Go get me a screwdriver, please. It's in the toolbox. It's the only orange one in there. I need it to get this belt tightened so we can start up the line and get this little beastie moving again. I see you making it back in about five minutes. Try not to get sidetracked, since every minute the line is down is costing us a fortune. Don't slip on the floor. Go for it. And thanks."

I count five types of visions. There's one for the organization as a whole — it's the big-picture one. Another is for a department or a function. One is for a person — a job description. The fourth is for a specific task. The last is situational, as in "Here's how we are going to handle this situation."

Sometimes we get very detailed, such as in the screwdriver assignment above. We do this when we are dealing with someone new. Sometimes, our approach is much more collaborative, where we talk things through with the person or group. This is when we have the time, the task requires a group-think approach, and, for various reasons, we want people involved. Sometimes the vision is somewhat one-sided, such as when we are announcing our new location to the employees.

SHIFTING THE FOCUS

Sometimes managers ask, "How can we give a vision to the troops if our own bosses don't tell us?" The question, I think, misses the point. Vision is meant to replace self-talk. If the troops are troubled by insecurity, we need to replace that self-talk with a more desirable kind. I have heard more than one successful manager stand in front of his team and announce something like the following:

> The fact is that I don't know exactly how the organization is going to tackle this monster. We all know we have a problem here. And I am confident that we will solve it. I have no idea how. But I'm not going to let that intrude on my thinking. I am going to choose to focus on the job. I sincerely want you to do the same. Don't get involved in worrying about it. You know your job well. Everybody in this room knows his or her job well. Whether this matter gets resolved or not does not affect our day-to-day jobs. I would like you to try to place your attention on the job. Face this challenge by gritting your teeth and doing as well as you can to satisfy our customers. Let's not lose track of what we do for a living around here.

This manager has attempted to replace his team's self-talk with a different one. He is trying to shift their focus. He has embraced not knowing the solution to the big problem and shown them a way out. This is leadership. We show them how to see the world. Otherwise, their own view just won't satisfy us.

One of the most fulfilling notions I have ever learned about is that just because we are having a thought doesn't mean that we have to go with it. Dogs and cats and rats and cows may have to go with whatever is mulling around in their brains, but humans don't have to. How empowering! If you are concerned about something, you can choose not to be. First you have to be aware of the concern. Then you have to decide whether to sustain it or not, and if not then you work to leave it alone. Managers help employees do that. We help them override their impulse to fall prey to their nagging self-talk.

As a public speaker, I have been saying to audiences for more than fifteen years that you can choose to be happy. I described visualizing little Shirley Temple singing "Just pick yourself up, brush yourself off, and start all over again." I described Norman Vincent Peale's *The Power of Positive Thinking* and encouraged audiences to try it. Admittedly, for the first five years of talking about it, I always thought it was easier said than done. I remember driving away from talks feeling sad about something, and thinking, "Okay, goofus, go ahead — think nice thoughts." I couldn't do it!

Then I learned a few more things. There is a trick that substantially helps one to override impulses. The trick is to practise doing things we don't like to do. For example, let's say you are walking somewhere and to get to your destination, you need to go up one floor. You have a choice: on the right is an escalator and on the left are the stairs. Assume for the moment that you are an escalator kind of person.

Well, take the stairs. Do that kind of thing several times a day — just little things that you don't really want to do but have the strength to choose to do. By choosing to override the impulse to take the escalator, you are practising your ability to override impulses. Your self-esteem temporarily rises as a result. Because there is an intimate link between self-esteem and will, by practising this overriding gesture, your sense of will climbs as well. Then, the next time you are feeling sad, rejected, worried, depressed, or negative in any way that you would like to override, you will have an improved ability to do so. (You have to catch the negative feeling early, though. Otherwise it hooks you and is harder to override.)

Part of the mechanics here is the notion of there being more than one self in our personalities. We comprise many parts. A wise man named Roberto Assagioli founded a whole form of psychotherapy on the idea, called psychosynthesis. If we let all our "selves" rule, nobody's in charge. But *we* can be in charge. You are the leader amongst the parts of your personality. And you are the leader amongst the members of your team. You are the agent. You are driving the bus. If you let everybody run around on their own, they may not cooperate. Sometimes you have to do what you don't want to do. Sometimes the people you lead have to do what they don't want to do.

So you ask your people to change their attitudes. You communicate to them that they can choose to feel bad about some current situation or they can put their attention elsewhere. You help them to see themselves. And as a result you help them to become, in a sense, different people — or the same people with different perspectives.

BUILDING COMMONALITY

You can't stand in front of your group and make announcements about how you want them to see the world unless you can psychically connect with them. You need to couple an ample supply of empathy with the renewed focus. Empathy is key, as we keep discovering.

There is a rule in sales that applies nicely here: "Build commonality before you lead." That is, we need to say things to make people feel heard before they will follow us. Press and release.

For example, here are two speeches with essentially the same content. Which one is more inspiring?

"I know that as you read this book you are keeping an eye out for what is useful for you and what is not. Sometimes you probably find yourself reading about a concept that you have trouble buying. It doesn't quite fit. And some of the times this happens to you, you probably choose to glide right past the concept. I strongly suggest you do yourself a favour in those moments. Slow down and try to spot the writer's message. Try to twist your world view to make it fit. Stop and reread where necessary to really capture the point being made — it might help you."

> "When people read books like this, they tend just to skip past parts they don't fully accept or understand. This is unwise because it causes them to miss the writer's point. What they should do instead is stop reading and think. They should try to find some validity in the message in order to take full advantage of what is available to them."

The point here is that empathy stops chatter. When you read the first speech, you probably followed along more closely. But reading the second speech you probably were doing some self-talk mumbling. Notice how with the first you were more involved in the content. That is empathy and focus in combination. Press and release.

In fact, when we communicate as leaders, we tend to be more effective when we move between the two poles. The following breakdown of a statement delivered by a leader illustrates this effective shifting between press and release.

Empathy or Focus	Step	Statement
focus *(press)*	introductory statement of broad expectation	Today I want to talk with you about the new system for handling projects.
empathy *(release)*	anticipating the thoughts of the listeners	A lot of you have expressed concerns about how much extra time the system will take. It's true the system will consume more time, and we all know how overworked we've been lately. It's a legitimate concern.

Empathy or Focus	Step	Statement
focus (press)	specific details of vision: time-bound, realistic, achievable, connected to the customer, specific, detailed	But the system in the long run is going to save us a lot of time and trouble. Here's how: . . .
empathy (release)	expected struggle	Undoubtedly, one challenge we all will face is the learning curve required. As you can see, at first glance this thing is like a monster. When you face this feeling, try to move past it. It'll go away.
focus (press)	restatement of key aspects of vision	I want everyone to have this first part mastered by the end of the quarter.
empathy (release)	anticipating private thoughts of listeners	As wicked as that seems, the good news is that it's doable. The pioneering work done by Bill shows that even a self-proclaimed computer doze like him can be fluent in less than a month.
focus (press)	confidence	I know we can do this and I look forward to sharing with you the advantages of the system. It will make our lives much easier.

Notice how the manager spent time anticipating the inevitable problems involved in fulfilling the vision. This is key, because when the team faces the obstacles that Murphy's Law anticipates, their self-talk, which might otherwise turn towards the negative, will instead sound like this: "The manager predicted this. And I know what to do."

REPEATING THE VISION

Another key to successfully keeping the team moving towards the goal is to repeat the vision regularly. You can't just expect to write a vision statement, make your announcement at a team meeting, and then sit back and relax. It's necessary every day. In a sense, this is what we do for a living, right? We get things done through other people. We work with them to define the objective and send them on their way. We meet regularly to check in. We keep people on track.

Some people lose focus more quickly than others, so we need to stay in touch more often. I know executives who are quite focused in their style. They are bright and capable of significant concentration. But they forget the big picture. They miss the forest for the trees. Life is like that. You discover what you believe in. You go out and start behaving appropriately. You get involved in a specific matter that is consistent with your personal vision. And suddenly you've lost the big picture.

This tendency is a good argument for why it's okay to state the obvious. For example, I could say to you: "Try your best to digest the contents of this book. I propose it has the potential to help you immensely."

Or I could give the following speech. Note how it states the obvious but still has the effect of grounding its recipients.

> Someday you are going to die. Between this day and that terrible day, I suspect that you want to experience maximum fulfillment. You want to be able to look back on your time as a manager and say that you were effective, that you helped people while achieving your own goals and those assigned to you. Well, my suggestion here is that the contents of this book can actually have a positive impact on this level of self-satisfaction. So try your best to digest the contents of this book.

No new information was brought to you in that statement other than that the author thinks this book can help you be a better manager. The extra wording was intended to keep you centred. And that is exactly why we don't hesitate in delivering our vision statements to restate things we have said and got agreement on before.

TROUBLESOME CHATTER FIVE

Earlier we saw that we can classify our employees in certain ways, such as by noting whether they are introverted or extroverted, and that recognizing these classifications helped us to tailor our management style to maximize our chances of being heard when we communicate. We also saw how we could use this knowledge of our people to make management decisions, such as where to physically locate people so that they were with similar personality types. We reached these conclusions about our employees basically by observing their behaviour. We could observe, for instance, that one person seemed to make his decisions based on feelings while someone else based her decisions on facts and logical reasoning.

There is another, perhaps more subtle but potentially more valuable method of getting to know our people. It involves recognizing patterns in their speech — in their verbalized self-talk. Sometimes the patterns we see in people's speech turn out to be to our management benefit. Sometimes, on the other hand, the patterns cause us problems. Our goal in this chapter is to recognize patterns to help us change them. Our goal is to coach people through problematic patterns so that they become more effective employees.

RECOGNIZING PATTERNS

I know a woman who seems to accept change more readily than anyone I have met. When she hears of yet another new direction to be pursued by her organization, a change that most of her colleagues squirm over, this woman embraces it. It's great.

Another positive pattern is when employees accept criticism without taking it personally. They don't get defensive. They readily recognize that it is a certain behaviour that is being criticized, not them personally. They know that they are not their behaviour. When misfortune occurs they seek solutions. These people are called agents. When managers are heard to declare "Don't bring me problems, bring me solutions!", they are begging their employees to become agents.

But there are myriad troublesome patterns as well. Some people handle criticism or failure terribly. When something bad occurs they busy themselves trying to deflect responsibility, declaring, "It's not my fault." These people are called victims.

Others announce optimistically that they will execute some grandiose plan that obviously captures the essence of something we all know they need to do in order to be substantially better at their job. It is clear that they understand exactly where they are weak — but consistently they let everyone down by not coming through.

Some people are naysayers, uttering the equivalent of "Nope, can't get there from here" with every request for help. They seem to close down, focusing instantly on why something can't be done rather than on how it might get done.

And then there are the generalizers. They frequently use words like "always," "never," "everybody," "nobody," "everywhere," "nowhere." They utter statements like: "We never plan"; "This company always makes that mistake"; "All generalizers are wrong." Of course, sometimes this tendency is good and sometimes it is not so good. I wouldn't mind a production person who had the instant reaction to new ideas: "We can do anything." I would be challenged by the salesperson who said "Every new product we make fails." A key point for generalizers is that their claims are rarely true.

Generalizing is a natural tendency, however. As a rule of thumb, if I see an electric stovetop, I don't lean on it. It's a guideline I have followed since childhood. The tendency helps animals survive. It helps us learn. In fact, as a manager, if you are adept at recognizing recurring behaviour, you will be more instructive in conducting coaching conversations. We'll look at that a little later in this chapter. Unfortunately, generalizations are also at the heart of prejudice. When the generalizing tendency gets in the way of opportunity, replaces rational thinking, or becomes hurtful to others, it's problematic.

Let's not forget the worriers, who jump to a "what if" mode. When misfortune is followed by fear because someone lets the question "What if this keeps happening?" rule their thinking, I think we have a problem. These people can let their fears impede their thinking.

Another common pattern shows up as a temper problem. People who use the word "should" a lot in their self-talk tend to get angry quite readily. The odds are that the next time you get angry you will notice the word "should" running through your personal chatter.

"I should have got that job." "This company should clean up its act."

It's important to distinguish between troublesome patterns that can be fixed and those that probably cannot. I may find it frustrating to work with "right-brain" folks who digress in conversation to some matter only indirectly related to what I think happens to be the topic under discussion. But this is not something I should aspire to change in them. It's who they are. Maybe I am the loony, overly focused on some goal as though it is the god of the day. The question in this particular case is whether the person is in the right job. If the role calls for creativity, maybe they are well suited to their job.

Similarly, perhaps the naysayer referred to above is more suited to an accounting role than a sales one. After all, wouldn't it be better to be protected financially by a person who saw why ventures would not work or why promises to pay warrant doubt than by a pie-in-the-sky risk-taking optimist?

The point, of course, is that you get to decide whether or not a certain pattern is conducive to the needs of the role, and whether it is a big problem or a small problem, and whether you can change it. If it is problematic for the role and looks impossible to change, then reconsider whether the person belongs in the role. If it is problematic in the person's relationship with you and with others, but in fact is well suited for the job the person is doing, then don't make any changes.

Things come in degrees, though. For example, a client asked me to help him address a concern shared by his sales force. It seemed that everyone in the sales team was complaining that the manager of the credit department was rejecting too many customer requests for credit. He was allegedly too much of a naysayer. Their view was that they were out pounding the pavement generating money-making opportunities for their company and when it came time to ship the product, the credit department was rejecting the customers. Credit's view was that the customers in question weren't worth the risk.

After several talks with the client, the credit manager, and the sales managers, it became clear: the company probably did need a naysayer in the role of credit manager, but this fellow was going overboard. He didn't need to be removed; he was simply ready for some minor tweaking in his decision and communication style.

Some psychologists consider how people reveal their self-talk in everyday conversation. Martin Seligman, for example, author of the book *Learned Optimism*, suggests that when a person explains a misfortune in their lives, they may reveal their self-talk. By spotting the words people use frequently, and by carefully listening to their messages for patterns such as those described above, you can detect tendencies in thinking.

Seligman says that when people respond to bad events in their lives, they may see the misfortune as being short-term or long-term, restricted to that unfortunate matter or likely to pervade other aspects of life as well, and their fault or not their fault. He suggests that people who see bad events as localized, temporary, and not their fault reflect optimism. Those who see a bad event as their fault, or as a reflection of their whole world falling apart, are being pessimistic. So too are people who let a bad event bother them for a prolonged period or who predict a misfortune will go on and on.

The point of the labels is that people, says Seligman, are more likely to be successful in life if they are optimistic. My suggestion to you is that if you can recognize negative patterns in an employee's chatter, and you can label it, whether with the pessimism label or just the generalizer label, then you can communicate your concern and help the employee to understand it and observe it in himself. And begin to change it.

I believe that employees who perceive themselves as victims of misfortune, placing blame everywhere but on their own shoulders, are less likely to be successful than others, and require, therefore, coaching by their leader. (This differs from Seligman's perspective, where people who deny blame are considered optimists and candidates for success.)

Those who have low self-esteem tend to do one of two things when misfortune occurs: they either get very down on themselves or they do the opposite and get very defensive and vehemently deny any blame. In this latter case they are protecting themselves lest their low self-esteem plummet further.

If a person takes the depressed route, he will tend to fail because he spends his energy on personal fault rather than on solutions. If he takes the route of strongly denying any blame, then he is also likely to fail because he does not look inward to discover what to do differently next time. My suggestion is that the optimist is the person who, regardless of fault, seeks solutions. If they play a role in misfortune, they plan personal adjustment without getting upset. If they perceive that they play no role in the problem, they plan external adjustment. This is the "agent."

ADDRESSING PATTERNS

If it is clear to you that you have an employee who exhibits a troublesome pattern in her behaviour and you think it is coachable, how do you do it? You either address it when it manifests itself or you address it in a somewhat more formal coaching conversation. In chapter 9 we shall look at a step-by-step agenda for conducting coaching conversations. For now, let's consider how to address them as they arise.

Let me make it clear that you are reading the words of someone who believes it is your responsibility to address troublesome patterns. Most managers I know have their own self-talk patterns that hold them back from addressing these issues. They ignore the problem. Or they recognize it, promise themselves they will address it, and let months go by without touching it. Or they save it for an annual review (and then the boss's boss wonders why this manager procrastinates on reviews).

The troublesome pattern you would like to address probably shows up in conversation. This is because when you have fairly close relationships with your employees you talk a lot. During your conversations, you will be able to discover many clues to a person's thinking patterns.

Victims, generalizers, those who say "I can't" or "what if," those who don't come through on their promises — or those who manifest any other problematic pattern — all benefit from having the pattern made clear to them. It has to be done tactfully, of course. In fact, one reason most of us are reluctant to address attitude problems with our employees is that those problems are so intangible. Often we see repeated signs of them but we don't know how to describe them, and we anticipate that our descriptions will be met with denial or offence.

When we address employee attitude problems it is important to avoid getting into heated debate. Dale Carnegie had a sweet and simple point about this. In his book *How to Win Friends and Influence People* he pointed out his belief that "you can never win the argument." If you think you won, then the other person feels he lost. You have deflated him and have therefore not really won at all. But we still want to raise the point. And we want to avoid a situation that goes something like this:

> *You:* Rickie, you've got an attitude problem.
> *Employee:* No, I don't.
> *You:* Yes, you do. You exhibit victim behaviour.
> *Employee:* No, I don't. Prove it.
> *You:* What about that report yesterday? It was late and all you did was give excuses.
> *Employee:* No, I didn't.
> *You:* Yes, you did.
> *Employee:* No, I didn't. I gave an explanation. You wanted to know what happened.

One rule of thumb I try to follow is to not go on quests with employees for the truth about their attitudes. It sounds terrible. But from my experience, every time I have cited examples of attitude problems, the conversation turns to whether the example qualifies as an attitude problem. Attitude problems are subjective judgments we make. They are not tangible things out in the real world that can be proven. They are always a matter of interpretation. For example, I interpret someone as always saying what cannot be done rather than what can; she interprets the same behaviour as honesty and provides evidence for why her assessment is accurate.

So I replace the quest for truth in this case with an effort to help the person with her personal packaging. It is a useful move. Essentially it means saying: "Regardless of the truth about this — because you may well be right — we still have a packaging issue here. And in business, packaging is important. So let's not spend our time debating whether it is true or not. Let's focus on how people viewing you in this way may hold you back from reaching your goals."

Communicating troublesome patterns also must be done in a way that maximizes understanding. There is a helpful model that can help us here. It is a model that I think has been slowly emerging in Western thought. It has been around in various forms in the East for millennia, but our Western reluctance to acknowledge the existence of self, let alone, for some, even consciousness, has retarded its arrival. In the last decade or so, particularly through the efforts of the psychological researchers dabbling in this new field of emotional intelligence, it has grown in acceptance.

It is the notion that people are more successful if they are aware of themselves and their reactions to the world. The awareness gives them more of an ability to manage their reactions. It takes the ability to be self as observer, observing self as the object of observation. Buddhists have been doing it for centuries. One Buddhist meditation involves alternating between being engaged in activity and being mindful or aware of the engagement. The activity elicits the same kind of "zone" that sports enthusiasts seek. It's somehow being aware and being engaged simultaneously, as though there is a witness standing on one's shoulders observing what one is doing and providing feedback.

Now I'm not saying that you or your employees need to engage in Buddhist philosophy or meditation. Indeed, the message is simply that you want your people to be aware of what's going on in their own heads, so that they can have control over their responses rather than just having them.

META-LEVEL THINKING

Your role begins with describing the pattern. Do it thoughtfully. The trick to causing the understanding, I think, is to encourage what one might call "meta-level" thinking. For example, rather than saying, "Bob, you just said that there's no way we can do it. Well, I think we can," say something like "Bob, often I think I hear you say that there's no way we can do it. You just said it there. You know, I think that's a kind of pattern in your responses. I'd like you to observe that pattern and let's talk about it again." Notice how the desirable approach encourages broad observation whereas the first version encourages simple local debate. In this case, meta-level thinking focuses on a prolonged period rather than a single incidence.

Another way to present meta-level thinking is to

place an issue under an umbrella category. For example, if you were concerned that an employee swears in front of customers, rather than saying, "John, don't swear in front of customers," you could say, "John, I'd like to talk about ways you can have an impact on customer satisfaction." Notice in this case how subsuming the issue under a heading that is slightly broader than the issue at hand encourages the meta-level thinking.

Encouraging meta-level thinking sets up a context for self-observation. The self doing the observing is at a higher level: it can see the bigger picture. That's what it's like to be self-aware. The agent who is doing the observing sees more than the single thing being observed — the agent sees the single thing in a broader context. By levying your criticism in this way, you provide a way for your employee to be that broad observer. In the temporal mode, we are saying, "From the point of view of someone who sees recurring events, notice, please, how this single occasion is a recurring thing." In the umbrella-concept mode, we are saying, "From the point of view of someone who sees the effect of behaviour, notice, please, how this single behaviour produces this certain effect."

One thing about meta-levels is that the higher level contains all that the lower levels contain and much, much more. It is just like the principle of dimensions. From the point of view of a dot, dotness is the whole world. But from the point of view of a line, a dot is a minor thing. It takes a whole lot of dots to make a line. To a plane, a line is trivial, just one little thing. To a line, a plane is almost unimaginable. It's a whole new dimension, a different game.

What we are doing when we set up meta-level thinking for our employees is allowing them to take pleasure in what their self contains. We are reminding them, in a sense, of the joys of being human. If a plane contains multiple lines, then, by analogy, we are reminding the plane of that fact. The observation of a single line is certainly within the plane's reach. It's a reminder of just how magnificent the plane really is. When we talk about patterns with people in this way we are helping them with their self-awareness. We are helping them have control over their patterned responses. Just pointing out an event or a single problem helps. But from my experience, meta-level delivery is much more powerful.

BLOCKING PATTERNS
AS THEY ARISE

Another way to address patterns is to block them when they arise. For example, if someone says, "We never do things right," you can respond with, "Never?" Or, if someone says, "All equipment like that breaks down," you can respond with, "All equipment?"

People who sustain the victim pattern are tougher to block. Recall that a victim is a person who deflects responsibility. "It's not my fault, boss; it's because of the following many things . . ." The best way I know to resist victim thinking is to have a conversation with the person and say something like this:

> Do me a favour. From now on in our relationship, if you believe that you can't do something that needs to be done, then come and tell me before it becomes a problem.

Also, here is rule number two: Never tell me we have a problem coming up — that is, unless you offer me solutions at the same time.

If we follow these two rules, I think you and I will be happy forever.

You don't have to be so glib in your delivery, but the method is clear and it works. The key is to encourage responsibility by making it against the rules to say, after a problem occurs, "It's not my fault." The new rule is that if you don't hear about problems, it means they were solved without your involvement. If you do hear about problems, it's only with possible solutions accompanying their delivery.

Victims can be tricky. After a deadline is missed or a problem arises, they may report that they didn't know something was going to go wrong because it was out of their hands. In this situation, we announce that when they are involved in a project, they are wholly responsible for it. They need to establish systems for themselves to advise them of impending problems in the same way that you have established the system of finding out in advance as well (by the two rules above).

Blocking the pattern of an employee who seems to mumble "I'm not happy here, I'm not happy here" is a tougher job than dealing with victims. But it is a pattern that needs to be addressed, because of the bad apple syndrome: the attitude can spread quickly and sour the whole group. There is a message that I like to send to people with this attitude, people who appear genuinely unhappy and who always seem to be complaining about it. The message derives from a philosophy I refer to as "first principles management" or "existential management." The message goes like this.

I assume that what you want from your life is some sort of fulfillment, some sort of happiness. You want to look back at the end of your life at your time here and see that you had fun, is that right? Well, you definitely don't seem to be having fun. So we have a problem here. I don't know why you put up with it. How can you spend so much of your life time not being happy? I mean, the moments of our life are so precious, and so rare, isn't it a waste to spend it so unhappily? I propose something. If you are going to stay here, then let's agree that you are only going to do so if you can make yourself happy doing so. The things you feel bad about probably are not going to change. So you either learn to be okay with them or you choose to leave — for your sake. What I mean by this is that you find a way to make all these bad things more okay with you or you are wasting your time here. Don't you agree? For your sake, don't you agree?

Of course, all of this is done with empathy. We press, yes. But we release as well.

MANAGING YOUR OWN SELF-TALK

W E have talked about the chatter of your employees, and how it is your responsibility as a manager to recognize and change their self-talk. But what about you? Does your own self-talk support your goals? Are you managing yourself? Of course, it would be victim thinking for you to place the responsibility on someone else's shoulders for helping you to modify your own self-talk. It is wise to assume that you must do it yourself.

A good start is to know more about where your self-talk comes from and how to decide whether it is serving you well.

ORIGINS OF SELF-TALK

It is safe to say that most of the traits possessed by any living thing are present because they serve the being in some way. Survival is the name of the game. When a living being possesses a trait that aids its survival, then it has a better chance of living long enough to create offspring. If the offspring inherit the same life-enhancing trait, then they too strengthen their chances of survival.

The mammalian limbic system is a perfect example of this phenomenon. It is the part of the brain that, among other things, dictates a fight-or-flight response. If an animal perceives a threat to its survival, then the limbic system engages and can cause the animal to flee or to stay and fight. If a dog perceives a threat, it may respond with anger. So too might a human. The difference is that humans can override their limbic responses and dogs cannot. A dog does not say, "I'm having a bad day, and this mood is going to wreck my day, so I think I will choose to override the feeling — I'll start whistling, that'll do it."

It's interesting that many humans don't override their feelings either. If you lose your temper, you become the anger. For a short while there is no self-observation at all. You are simply lost in the emotion; for a short while you are unable to think "I'm losing my temper right now." Only after the limbic system calms a bit are you able to observe yourself: "I am angry right now." Once the word "I" makes it into your thinking, you are starting to be able to separate yourself from the anger. As more time passes you may still feel the anger but you are further away from it: "I have this anger inside me." By this point, you have moved from being the anger, to identifying yourself with the anger, to possessing anger but not being it, to simply remembering it.

The saving grace for humans is the cerebral cortex, a part of the brain that lower animals don't possess. Our thinking brain is capable of "seeing" or being aware of limbic impulses. At the point when you can declare, "I am angry," you have introduced your cerebral cortex into the situation. You may still be caught in the anger, but at least you are more than simply lost in the experience of it.

In fact, the more time your cerebral cortex spends on "seeing" the anger, the more your limbic system calms down. This is why we go to therapists, right? We talk through our confusing feelings so that we are finally separate from them. We leave the therapist's office still having the feelings, but we are no longer lost in them, identified with them. We have experienced "disidentification."

Presumably, self-talk occurs in the cerebral cortex. It's muttering away to itself all the time, observing the inside and outside world. And it's busy judging what it sees. If it judges something to be favourable to its survival, then it sends a positive message to the brain. If it judges something to be unfavourable, the message to the limbic system may be, for example, to run, or to fight, or to grieve.

Chatter is like a program that is always mulling over whether the events in the outside world are serving us well or not. Essentially it serves the same purpose as the set of nerves measuring pleasure and pain. A pin prick sends a pain signal to the brain alerting us to a possible threat. In the same way, a self-talk judgment of danger ahead sends a signal to the animal brain alerting us to a possible threat. Physical pleasure works the same way. Its mental correlate is a positive emotion.

When I was a child, I was walking home from school one day and was chased by a monster dog (twelve feet tall, I'm sure). The dog caught up to me and bit me. He hung on to my arm and swung me around while I made wailing cries of fear that could be heard throughout the neighbourhood. I then saw the owner of the dog running towards us. He was taking his belt out of his pants while running. I was sure he was going to hit one of us — perhaps me for making the dog mad, or maybe the evil dog itself. It was a terrifying situation.

But magic things were happening in my nervous system while all this was going on. It was rapidly installing a brand-new self-talk program that still engages today. The programming reads something like this: "From now on, when you see a dog — any dog will do — assume it's a problem." The system works. Speaking somewhat glibly, it is safe to say that dogs won't be causing me any problems for a while, since I basically feel the clear impulse to reject their company. When I see one, my self-talk says, "There's a problem; all dogs are evil." My self-talk is doing its job. It is protecting me from perceived threats to my survival. It receives messages about what is being perceived in the outside world, searches its memory bank for any record of similar things, and, more or less, makes its judgment.

The problem, of course, is that not all dogs need this reaction. Our self-talk makes mistakes. It does not base opinions on truth or reason. It lacks the time to work things through. It sends messages based on its programming. My job, I suppose, is to teach it to stop generalizing about dogs. The rule should not be that all dogs are evil. It should be that twelve-foot dogs might be a problem.

I know a fellow who had a sad childhood experience. He was invited to play spin-the-bottle with his grade seven classmates. Early in the game a pretty girl spun the bottle and it rested pointing at him. According to the rules, she had to kiss this fellow. But instead, she declared, "I'm not kissing him, he's dirty."

The poor fellow grew up with more than his share of subsequent rejection by people he wanted to befriend. Now he's in sales. People reject him regularly — it's part of his job. And it hurts. Every time. His self-talk became programmed over time to mumble to himself repeatedly, "Nobody wants me, I'm no good." This chatter not only makes him misinterpret what people are saying when they say no to products but it has caused him to predict their rejection. As a result his energy level is low, his posture reveals low self-esteem, and his tone of voice reflects his depression.

Again, his self-talk, with the best of intentions, is not serving him well. It's doing its job, but it does not help him achieve his goals. He sought help to develop his ability to override his self-talk and ultimately replace it with different self-talk. This would allow him not to be overwhelmed when people said no and to change his attitude as he anticipated approaching customers.

JUDGING AND CONTROLLING OUR OWN SELF-TALK

What kind of self-talk problems do managers face? Plenty. One of the most common self-management problems I see among managers is their reluctance to confront people problems. They have problems with employees but they don't want to correct them because of, for example, some perceived threat. Their self-talk says things like "It's a drag dealing with defensive people," or "I hate telling people what they do wrong," or "I can wait out problems like this." The list is as long as the number of managers who have the problem.

Then there are managers who are reluctant to talk to their bosses because of self-talk that questions their self-worth. Others say, "Planning never works." I've frequently heard "Training never works." I'm beginning to get negative self-talk about people I hear say, "You can't get good help these days," "Schools are a waste of time," "They just don't listen," "Youth today!"

Of course, maybe some of these observations are accurate. Maybe they are not. The issue is whether programmed perspectives hold us back from reaching our goals. If they do, we may want to change them. If they do not, then they are doing no harm, even if they are incorrect observations of the world.

But how can we override a lifetime of pattern recognition? It's not easy, but it's possible. And it's very useful.

First of all, deeply ingrained self-talk phrases are harder to override or reprogram. Somebody seriously neglected as a child is going to have a tougher time overcoming self-talk that sustains low self-esteem than someone who faced boyfriend rejection in her teens. Both individuals may have negative self-talk, but one internal conversation will likely be tougher to amend.

Another thing to keep in mind is that how long we have been reinforcing self-talk phrases partially determines how easily we may change them. We spend our lifetimes developing new perspectives and reinforcing old ones. Newer points of view are more easily overcome.

Of course, we only want to trouble ourselves with self-talk that interferes with our goal fulfillment. For example, if you have self-talk that makes you vulnerable to rejection, but you don't feel that it affects your ability to hit your goals, then there may be no need for you to address it. Perhaps you simply accept your vulnerabilities and are happy to live with them. Perhaps any problems ensuing from your vulnerabilities occur so rarely that changing your self-talk is not worth the trouble.

If, however, some self-talk *is* troublesome, the first thing to do is to become more aware of it. Catch yourself entertaining the problematic perspective. Then, assuming you have caught it soon enough, and it does not cause too severe an emotional response, you can override it.

For example, let's say you are a sales manager. One of your employees enters the room complaining that some people in another department have once again said something to a customer that negatively affects the performance of your own area. You shake your head and say to the employee, "Those people in credit just don't get it, do they? We have products to move, and they are naysayers for a living. You can't run a business by pushing customers away. They are always overreacting. I can't stand it." You pick up the phone and call the guilty party, alleging the disrespect you hold for their attitude towards customers and the health of the organization.

Well, we know that if you are deeply immersed in your limbic response that you are not even aware of what you are doing until some time passes. When you can catch an objective wave, it makes sense to ask yourself, "Is this going to help me get me what I want?" If it will really help in the long run, then go for it. If you conclude that it will not help, then you have a tremendous opportunity not only to change what you are currently involved in saying and doing but also to change your style. You've spotted a self-talk utterance worth amending.

Of course, as sales manager, your mission is to sell to as many customers as possible. The credit department has the job of saying no to as many bad risks as possible. It's a common tension that organizations build right into the system. Let them battle it out, senior people say, knowing that if they both do their jobs, things will work out. The problem is that in the scenario described, you are actually hurting yourself. By being so aggressive with your counterparts in credit you are alienating them. This might make them less reasonable in their analyses of credit viability. Out of spite, the credit department might say no to people who in fact deserve the right to buy inventory on credit.

So, either during the conversation with the guilty department, or in advance of a subsequent conversation, you take step one: you ask yourself, "What is my self-talk here? What am I saying to myself?" As we saw in a previous chapter, the word "should" is probably present. Perhaps you find running through your head: "Nobody should step in my way; anybody getting in my way gets stepped on, hard and fast."

After detecting this pattern of self-talk, you can change it on the spot: "The people in credit are doing their job — it's a good thing too, because if they didn't, we would probably ram too much through the doors." With the revised self-talk engaged, a call to sort out the individual case would be less likely to evoke a defensive posture from the credit department and everything is back on track.

One of the keys, clearly, is to catch the negative self-talk before it engages the limbic system. Once we are already pulled in, it is difficult to control self-talk to quell the anxious feelings. It is easier for self-talk to override other self-talk than it is for self-talk to take control of the wild animal within us.

Once you have caught the negative thinking, it is time to change it. If a generalization is present, it begs for attention. As we saw in the last chapter, generalizations are rarely true. If the word "should" is there, you know that is probably not useful either. "What if" scenarios probably aren't useful either, since they evoke a worry response. The word "can't" is often limiting because it creates the belief that things are just not possible. A judgment about what people must be like for having done something is also self-talk that could be adjusted, since it is surely their *behaviour* we want to judge, not them as people. Basically, the rule for assessing your self-talk is to question the judgments you have made.

As soon as you have replaced the phraseology, you will probably notice some dwindling of emotional verve; once your cerebral cortex intervenes with a rational perspective, the limbic system relaxes. Again, this assumes that you have caught the old pattern in time. If not, you may have to wait until the next time around. But headway has still been made, because you have practised exercising your awareness of the problem.

The next challenge is to embed the new, healthy chatter as deeply as you can. Repetition is key. Even in the 1700s, teachers knew about the value of making someone repeat certain phrases in order to change behaviour. My son was recently struggling with an impending mathematics exam. He was finding it difficult to sit down and practise math questions. His self-talk was something to the effect of "I can't do math." As far as I was concerned, his attitude about the math was more of a detriment to his chances of success than whatever his skill limitations might have been. I proposed the repetition route.

As terrible as it sounds, I had him write out several hundred times, "It's not whether I pass or fail, it's how I attack the subject." My mission was to take his attention away from where it seemed to want to go — his math skills — and put it on attitude alone. I believe the shift worked, although it seemed somewhat invisible to my son. Within hours of the treacherous writing exercise I spotted him diving into practice questions. At least the change allowed him to override his self-limiting attitude and let him reap some advantage from practising questions he was weak at.

I have seen repetition work in other ways as well. As a personal coach for managers I have the pleasure of weekly meetings with people who are wrestling certain problems down over time. By meeting with them regularly and repeating a primary message — such as "Addressing employee problems directly doesn't hurt me, it actually makes things better" — I have observed people breaking out of self-imposed limitations.

For example, one executive I worked with was vehemently disliked by her direct employees. They considered her cold and impersonal and resented her "inhuman" style. After speaking with the executive, I learned that she was aware of the problem but had no idea of the cause. We got her self-talk out on the table, so to speak, and on the topic of communication her perspective went like this: "My people are busy, they have no time to waste; they just want the facts." She was assuming that this was how people wanted to be treated. She didn't realize they also wanted to be recognized for doing good work — for being people.

But the intellectual realization that she was missing a key point about employee needs didn't quite make the difference. She was not able to amend the self-talk overnight. We had to role play, for ten or fifteen minutes, once a week for two months, before we both agreed that a new habit was forming. Interestingly, the self-talk phrase she chose to adopt to correct her attitude projection — and it was her creation, not the consultant's — was: "This person is going to die some day; how sad." Her choice, though perhaps a tad morbid, brought out her compassion. With practice, it did replace her original, well-programmed approach.

Another way to change personal self-talk is to write in a diary or journal. By forcing ourselves to engage our cerebral cortex to articulate troublesome points of view, we wind up employing a private therapist — ourself. In the process we gain enough distance from our problematic perspective to see our problem but be less emotionally encumbered by it.

One of my favourite ways to get past negative chatter is to simply spend time with people who don't have it. You undoubtedly spend your time with people who share your negative point of view on certain matters. My advice: choose the company of others. Self-talk can change when you don't hear it shared — reinforced — by others.

Motivational tapes also have the ability to override conditioned points of view. We allow the speaker to enter our thinking subliminally. Even without listening consciously to the speaker's message, we can absorb it. My experience has been that if we listen to a tape with a message we respect, it can affect our mood substantially.

Sometimes we can override negative self-talk by yelling to ourselves. I know someone who quit smoking this way. He would drive in his car and loudly admonish himself, as though he was a parent using screaming to discipline a child: "You disrespectful little liar! You committed to me that you would quit smoking and you lit up another one! Have you no integrity? I can't stand you like this!" and so on. Apparently, four private sessions with himself was all it took.

Of course, more-positive messages can be transmitted this way as well. I once observed a video-based sales training session conducted by Lee DuBois in which he got an entire audience to rise from their seats and yell out, at the top of their lungs, the words "I am!" in answer to his staged question, "Who is the greatest salesperson in the world?" The effects were remarkable.

Sometimes I use a version of the same instructional tool when presenting to large audiences. I ask them to record a number between one and ten that reflects how they feel at that moment. "It's a secret number," I say. "Nobody will ask you what you write, just make it an honest reflection of how you feel right now, being here in this room. The number five represents indifference, zero is verging on suicide (so see me after class), and ten is orgasm." Then I pose a question similar to Mr. DuBois's. Everybody rises, yells a brief response, claps their hands once, and sits down. Usually I come back by showing some disappointment in the crowd's lack of fast, loud response and drag them through the process again. Sometimes it's again and again. After repeating the exercise until everybody is both frustrated with the nuisance and laughing at the process, I quickly say:

"Okay, now pick up your pencils and write a new number." People laugh. They record their mood, and I ask for a show of hands from those whose number rose. Consistently, more than 80 percent raise their hands. The exercise is a great way of showing how we can override self-talk.

Of course, many things affect the mood elevation that takes place in this scenario. And they all affect self-talk. The fact that the audience didn't want to play in the first place, that it involved physical activity (rising from their seats, clapping their hands), that the message was positive, that other people were doing the same thing, and that they were yelling the positive phrase — all contributed to the control over self-talk.

There are many other ways to gain control of self-talk. But every effort to do so has the same goal in mind: to interrupt one programmed response in order to replace it with another point of view that is more conducive to achieving our goals. After all, we wouldn't want to be victims of our programming. We seek instead to be agents, taking responsibility for our interpretation of what happens around us.

WHO IS MANAGING WHOM?

SEVEN

NOT all our self-talk is programmed by our life experiences. There is reason to believe that some of our programming is congenital. For the sake of species survival we are presumably born programmed to respond to specific stimuli. Just as our self-talk gets rolling if some reminder of a childhood trauma occurs, so does it get charged up if some trigger that the nervous system innately recognizes as good or bad for survival occurs.

The programming works just as reflexes do. If you raise a hand to strike me, I might wince and shield my face from your blow — a natural reaction. The sound of a crying baby can be a terrible one for adult humans to hear — it can create mass anxiety because everyone within hearing range wants to act and, perhaps, cannot. Or when we think that something important will be in short supply, we are inclined to replenish our supplies. We are "hardwired," if you will, to respond to these perceptions; it preserves the species.

Employees and events around us push our buttons all the time, and we may not be happy with the consequences of our response. For example, we may be tempted, against our logic, to retain an employee who is threatening to leave our organization. Something deep inside might be driving us to persuade the person to stay when in fact our rational mind might know better. This would be the result of the compliance principle of scarcity — the tendency to avoid running out of things we "think" we need. The tendency can easily be wrong.

Self-talk and compliance responses are not the same thing. Self-talk comes from repeated interpretations of life events — interpretations fed to us by parents, other people around us, the media, and, as we develop, ourselves. Compliance responses derive from a deeper level of mental activity.

We will look at eight stimulus-response patterns in this chapter. They all are relevant for managers. They help us to know when we are being clear-headed in our behaviour and when we are falling prey to deeper programs in our psyche. For our purposes, it is easiest to consider these various patterns in terms of "self" and "other."

The four stimulus-response patterns looked at from a self-oriented position are the impulse to fulfill our self-concept; the impulse to avoid shortage; the impulse to avoid negative consequences that we believe will come our way if certain conditions exist; and the impulse to pursue goals. Employees, suppliers, superiors, peers, and the marketplace generally all position things to take advantage of our tendencies to act in accordance with these programmed responses. It's up to us to decide what to do — we don't want to simply act out of impulse all the time.

From an other-oriented position, we experience the herd instinct, whereby learning that others do a certain thing will sometimes (mistakenly) lead us to do that same thing. Also, when we have rapport with people, we tend to comply with their wishes. Third, we feel indebted to people who have done things for us. In the fourth response, we tend to comply with the proposals of people we respect.

FULFILLING OUR SELF-CONCEPT

Let's say you go through an exercise with your team and conclude, "What we do for a living around here is manufacture widgets — we do it well, and we are proud of our work." You get everyone on your team to place their hands on their chests and declare the corporate oath to believe in and fulfill the mission. You go way out of your way to reiterate the mission, because you want everyone to see you supporting it.

Then an opportunity comes along — you are invited to distribute with your widgets the special little connectors that customers use to secure their widgets. You have a team meeting. The opportunity looks good — after all, you are delivering your widgets to the same customer; why not throw the connectors into the carton and make a few bucks on the side? But you and the team think better of it. "No," you agree, "we know what our business is. There's no way we are going to muddy our clarity. We manufacture widgets — we are not a distributor of widget products!" The decision is made and proudly declared: "No connectors." Everyone applauds your leadership. You are proud of yourself.

But your competition picks up the idea. Suddenly, they are seen as being more serious about serving customers. They've learned to bundle their products. They're more competitive. Your business is hurt, and all because of the stubbornness of a deeply ingrained belief that we must be what we are and we must not revoke our commitments.

This is not to say that we shouldn't define who we are. Indeed, in chapter 4 we addressed our need to give a clear sense of direction to the troops. But we must remain flexible enough to bend when a rational analysis reveals that being stubborn is being detrimental.

There is a much more surface-level example of this principle. So many times I have seen managers stand behind their word to their own detriment. For example, if they promise an office to Rickie and an office becomes available, then, even if there is a better use of the space, Rickie gets it because it was a promise. Rather than helping Rickie understand that things change, we might be inclined to (irrationally) behave consistently with our promise. Don't think that I espouse breaking promises. The decision to let Rickie down cannot be made lightly. After all, society is partially based on mutual trust and the fulfillment of promises. But our job is to do what is best for the organization we lead. If the downside of reneging is greater than the upside of pursuing another option, then sticking with the promise is the right answer. This chapter is about the wisdom of the analysis.

So the next time you feel compelled to fulfill your self-concept or your intentions to act in a certain way, it may serve you to ask yourself if the impulse comes from a rational place or a deeply ingrained propensity to do what you intended. Sometimes, changing gears, breaking out of the box, is the smart thing to do.

AVOIDING SHORTAGE

The second stimulus-response pattern that comes to light when we are in a self-oriented mode concerns the tendency to avoid shortage or loss. Were a caveman to awaken, notice his pile of apples dwindling, and ignore the observation, he would surely not survive. We tend to press our buttons when we run short on supply.

Have you ever found yourself looking for a product in a couple of stores, unable to find it, and, as a result, going somewhat overboard in your quest to acquire it? You want what you want when you want it. It's very common. And it can hurt you in business, such as when we negotiate. Out of the fear of losing a deal with a customer, we feel inclined to satisfy customer demands, forgetting that the customer needs or prefers to do business with us. This tendency causes us to lower prices rather than sell our way out of fiscal problems.

Time after time I have listened to sales managers lament how their salespeople return from customer meetings with pleas for lower prices. "We'll lose the business otherwise," they say. Giving in to these pleas can lead to the demise of the organization. I have more often seen organizations survive by increasing their prices than by lowering them. Fear of loss can push our buttons.

It reminds me of my own consulting activities. I started out charging $35 per hour, thinking it was a little steep. I raised this fee rate, nervously gritting my teeth, to $45 per hour. When nothing happened, I entered the big leagues by leaping to $65 per hour. My goodness, I thought, even that had no effect. In fact, it seemed to create this curious desire from customers to grant me more credibility. That was a key message. From there it went to $75 and then $95. The customer hunger for more of me seemed to rise even further. With every new project, I kept raising the fee: as I became more scarce, or was perceived to be scarce, the more I could get. Nowadays it has become so absurd I feel inclined to stop raising it out of some principle. (Really it's some other deeply ingrained limiter in my own head, a form of social reciprocity — but is it rational?)

Fear of shortage pushes our buttons. Next time you apply for a job, ask for more vacation time than they offer. Giving it to you is so easy, and losing you by saying no seems so scary, they'll likely say yes. By the same token, the next time someone asks you for more, think about whether the impulse to give in comes from a rational cost/benefit risk analysis, or whether it comes from your irrational fear that the person might leave the company if you take a firm stand.

FEARING NEGATIVE CONSEQUENCES

The third patterned impulse is similar to the fear of shortage response, except that rather than fearing the loss of what we want, we fear some other negative consequence. This is common in the form of "fear of confrontation." We don't like discomfort. We don't like to fight. So we tend to avoid such situations.

Think of one of your more troubling employees. Wouldn't you say you have a problem that you probably should confront sooner than later? But rather than dealing with our messes, we often just avoid them, irrationally. The smart thing to do is to override the fear and address our problems so that we can make things better.

PURSUING GOALS

The tendency to move towards our goals is the opposite of the previously described tendency. We tend to do things when we perceive that doing them will help us to get what we want. This tendency is at the heart of focused thinking. Half of this book is about this human tendency. Out of our desire to reach goals, we do what seems like the logical thing. We remove obstacles, use resources, make and implement plans. We use the tendency to our advantage when we communicate rationally with our employees. We help them see where we are going and make it clear how it is a good place to go. We influence them by painting a picture of our destination and drawing up clear plans for reaching it with minimal pain.

But the tendency backfires when something we think is rational is in fact not. If an employee presents what looks like a logical argument to do a certain thing, we may agree just because of the alluring appearance of cogent thinking. As we will see in the next chapter, the way to assess a proposal is to ensure that the goal is clearly defined, all the obstacles that can be conceived of are addressed, all the resources available have been considered, and the plan can be efficiently implemented. Approving ideas that do not go through a rigorous process like this can be tempting — after all, we want what we want — but irrational.

Now it is time to consider the reactions we have to certain stimuli that occur when we are in an other-oriented mode. These involve other people. Our receptiveness to their opinions can make us do things that, in our better minds, we may not think we should do.

HERD INSTINCT

When we learn that others are doing something, we often feel the impulse to do it ourselves. For example, if the competitors are throwing in free backrubs with every purchase, we may feel inclined to throw them in as well. When an employee says that lots of companies are putting web pages on the Internet, we may feel inclined to copy the decision to keep up — not because it is necessarily the right thing to do.

The problem with following the herd is that it can be counter to the whole marketing notion of differentiation. The trick is not just to catch up with our competitors, it is to surpass them. After all, if we do what everyone else does, what makes us different? If we do what everyone else does, what makes us better? Our tendency to trust what others do can limit us.

My consulting firm has clients who ask us to do things because they have heard that others do them. Their decision is not rational. Even though we declared our position about this, and we demonstrated proof for our position at the outset, they don't want to miss the boat. "Let's do it, just in case" is their response. "After all, it's not a trend for nothing."

RAPPORT

The second other-oriented stimulus-response pattern is our inclination to do what is proposed by people we like. This human tendency is a big part of many business decisions. For example, we tend to enjoy the company of those who are similar to us, so when we hire, we are more inclined to offer the job to someone who is just like we are. Of course, the problem with this is that the job being filled may require someone who is different from us.

I know a man who is very unfocused in conversation. He is creative, to be sure, but he wanders all over the place when you talk to him. Everybody he hires is exactly the same way — very divergent in thought and conversation. The problem is that some of the people he has hired have to deal with highly convergent-thinking customers for a living. They are the wrong people for the job. Yet my acquaintance misses this point when he hires. And he engaged a consultant to determine why customer service was suffering. "My people are all so friendly and creative! How could customer service be our problem?" He interviews job candidates and hires those with whom he has rapport. His mistake is in forgetting that customers may not have the same instant rapport with these people.

Another manager I know is as friendly as can be with his employees. They love him and he loves them. Whenever they ask him for things, he tends to give in. Friends do favours for friends all the time. Even he would readily admit that pretty much nobody is really running his company: "It's a tremendous team effort." The problem is that he can't say no to his team members. His decisions suffer as a result.

INDEBTEDNESS

We are also influenced by reciprocity, the principle that when people do things for us, we are obliged to return the favour. I know managers who don't remove people from positions that are not being satisfied just because they feel they owe the person. "She's worked so hard for us, it would be a shame to act on the problem.

We're hoping it will work itself out — she won't be here forever."

Because of reciprocity, smart employees wait to ask for favours after they have earned your favour. It makes sense, doesn't it? When else should we ask for a favour, other than when one is owed to us? The moral of the reciprocity story is that we need to be sure that our decisions are based on reason rather than on indebtedness. I may be smart to grant someone time off after she has worked hard on a successful project — not because I owe it to her, but just because the time off might give her time to recharge her batteries.

RESPECT

The last example of when we are influenced unduly occurs when we act because someone who is an alleged expert tells us to. Just because someone writes a book does not mean they are any good. Just because a consultant proposes that we act in a certain manner does not mean that it is better than our own inclination.

I have a client who pays handsomely for my opinion. He very rarely acts on what I propose, however. He says he simply wants the "expert" point of view so that, if he is going to make a "mistake," at least he'll do it knowingly. Thank goodness there are multiple ways of handling a challenge; otherwise, the logical conclusion would be that he is paying me for the bad advice I presumably must be giving so regularly.

All of the responses we have looked at relate in some way to the survival of the species. That's why we have them. We do what the herd does because the herd is not dead and it does a certain thing — presumably we won't die by doing it either. We make friends with people and follow their lead, presumably because humans do better hanging around with others of similar kind than they do out on their own. Feeling indebted to those who have done favours for us helps the species sustain a community of cooperating beings. All eight of the stimulus-response patterns link to genetic predisposition.

When we decide whether any particular programmed response is not suiting us well, we can override the response. Ideally, we are sufficiently in touch with ourselves that we will be able to say, "I think my response here is inconsistent with my rational goals. I think I need to override my impulse and adopt a different response." The overriding is carried out in the same manner as when we override self-talk responses. Our rational mind, able to see itself operating from a higher level, says, "Oh, look down there, my animal instincts are tricking my better judgment. It's time to step in."

To summarize what has been said in this chapter, here are some straightforward prescriptions.

- If someone alleges to be an expert, don't automatically take his advice. Make sure it's rational.
- If you feel you should do something because everybody else is doing it, reconsider.
  Ask yourself if it will harm the way you are different from the rest. Make sure it is rational.
- If someone asks for something and you feel you owe it to her, fulfill the debt only if it makes sense. Don't go around ignoring your debts; just watch the impulse to fulfill them — you may be ignoring a bigger picture.

- When someone you enjoy proposes a certain thing, don't let your enjoyment of the person intrude on your thinking.
- When someone makes what sounds like a logical proposal for how you can get what you want, check the logic.
- When you feel yourself aware of possible bad consequences of pursuing something, don't back down from pursuing it. Maybe charging forward is a smarter, more rational thing to do.
- If somebody tells you that things are in short supply — time, money, availability of widgets — and you feel the impulse to give in, watch out. You might be smarter to wait.
- If someone is reminding you that you must do something because you said you would do it, don't just jump at it. Maybe waiting a little longer can work. If you are confronted by an opportunity to break out of the box and you feel resistant, think things through. Maybe even close your eyes and jump.

Notice how all these bits of advice consume time? That's because the impulses they resist tend to make our life easier. We fall prey to mass opinion because in this world we don't have the time it takes to research things thoroughly. We jump at the advice of experts because doing so seems to bring a higher probability of success as well as saving us the time required to do our own research. We do things that fulfill our commitments and our self-concept because it is easier to stay within the paradigm that works than it is to break out of it.

All of the impulsive reactions can be seen on two levels: they help the species survive and they buy us time. But our job as rational managers is to make sure that our reliance on these reactions does not intrude on our ability to think through them and find better answers.

FOCUS EIGHT

WE have talked so far about how to help people replace their self-talk with a team vision that is acceptable to you. We have also talked about how to get people to replace their troublesome self-talk with more productive patterns of chatter. These are both examples of how to bring people who are wandering astray back on a track defined by you. But we have not yet addressed how you as the leader are supposed to think.

We know leaders ideally seek controlled, balanced levels of empathy and focus. But focus towards what? What does it mean to be focused? How do people who are focused tend to behave?

Surely you have noticed that throughout this book dualities have been recurring: focus and empathy, self-oriented and other-oriented, press and release. Some that have not arisen, but are tempting to entertain, are yin and yang, logical and emotional, left-brain and right-brain, inward and outward. These pairs have things in common, but they are not at all synonymous. "Self" and "other" may be the best pair of words to start a mini-analysis of what is going on here. They depict what I believe are the two modes of attention that lie at the heart of managers managing their own heads. The claim is that, as a manager, it is at times appropriate to dominate and at others it is appropriate to subordinate yourself in deference to the other person.

There are many reasons for why we need some balance here, rather than just being on top all the time. One selfish reason (it's hard to break away, isn't it?) is that you might derive value from placing your attention on something other than what you want. Another reason might be labelled the "moral" thing to do; after all, we are not alone in the universe — we've got to think about society. Another reason it is good to be other-oriented, and this one is selfish too, is that if you are not, then you will be less likely to win others over. Another is that it might be quite natural to attend to others. If we didn't have the tendency to love others, the species might not survive.

The key is that we benefit from orienting ourselves on purpose. Most of us don't balance ourselves optimally. This book is partly about making the right choices in this regard, about choosing what goes on in our consciousness rather than just letting it happen.

The terms "press" and "release" are meant to be approximate correlates. When we press upon the world we are being self-oriented. We are dominating. When we release, we are not. The "release" side of the pair doesn't quite possess the other-oriented connotation, the compassion sense — it just says we are not pressing. On the other hand, it might be argued that when we are not pressing, we are relaxed and open, ready to take in the pressing of others.

"Empathy" possesses the compassion. It is truly other-oriented. It takes a subordination of the self in deference to the other. "Focus" is a visual word that implies bringing something to the centre of attention. Usually managers focus on goals. And that activity is one of dominance. I know managers who are so dominant that even when they claim they are being other-oriented they are simply pressing. They might be heard to utter, while tapping their feet, gritting their teeth, and wringing their hands, "You want compassion? I'll show you compassion. Everybody watch out, I'm going to show compassion!" This is very probably not empathy — not until the toes stop tapping.

Whose goals do effective managers focus on? Therein lies the beauty of the term. "Focus" is a versatile word. Nobody is dictating what goes into our field of vision except we ourselves. All of us choose what to focus on. The object of focus is a target, a goal. Company goals, personal goals, employee goals, long-term goals, short-term goals, they all qualify. Effective managers are either dominating, pressing as they pursue goals, or in some sense shutting off their self-orientation and simply attending outwardly, empathizing. They choose their option.

Let's look at some examples. Let's say you are reading a memo written by someone on your team. If you are in an empathy mode, you are relaxing your goal-orientation and letting yourself absorb the perspective of the author. If you are in a focus mode, you are probably bringing judgment into your reading.

The same goes for a face-to-face conversation. If you are busy judging what you are hearing, you are probably, during the moments of judging, in a self-oriented mode. The act of judging in this sense is one of comparing what you are hearing to some goal you have in mind. When what you are hearing is conducive to the goal, you judge what you are hearing to be good. When it is counter to the goal, what you are hearing is not good. That's what makes it self-oriented. It's not that the goal necessarily concerns you, it is that you are doing the judging. Empathy, on the other hand, is judgment free.

Many managers mistakenly equate being quiet with being other-oriented or empathetic. If you are judging, you're in a self-oriented mode. If you are present, quiet, and not listening, you are in a self-oriented mode. Empathy means identifying with others. Focus implies being busy with some goal.

Effective managers are focused probably a little over half the time they are working in the presence of other people. Goal-orientation is infused into their thinking. In conversation, they tend to be heading somewhere. Efficiency is very relevant to their world view. They are rational.

Rationality is obviously of great importance in business. Something can be said to be rational if it helps to reach a goal efficiently. If the goal is to get a cup of coffee, doing anything that leads to having a cup of coffee does not make it rational. For example, if there is an acceptable cup of coffee in front of me, and I decide to go to the doughnut shop to get a cup of coffee, doing so would not be rational. It would be much more rational to grab the cup in front of me. Not drinking it when it was a goal and was available would also not be rational. Rationality is about efficiently reaching goals.

Other than being creative in their effort to generate new ideas for products or systems, rationality is a modus operandi for businesspeople. Focused managers thrive in the environment. We want to make money efficiently. As much money as we can. Spending as little as possible. In as short a time as possible. Generally, we try to maximize volume and maximize efficiency.

So the sequence goes like this: We set a *goal*. We try to minimize the *obstacles* that prevent us from reaching our goal. We try to maximize the *resources* available to us. And we make a *plan* that uses the resources to overcome the obstacles and reach the goal with minimum cost, in minimum time. Then we *implement*. After we have begun, we *check in* to see that we are on track. Also along the way, we try not to leave messes behind so that we don't make reaching the next goal more difficult.

FOCUSING ON GOALS

It all starts with goals. Even if there is no goal, the goal is to find a goal. To find a goal, one might ask oneself, "What's holding me back from defining the goal?" The answer will move things forward. We could even proceed, all with the goal of producing a goal, to ask ourselves what resources are available to help define the goal or overcome the obstacles to defining one. With these things in mind, we would make a plan to make a goal — only to start the process again in an effort to fulfill the goal. It's all very beautiful, yes?

Focused people handle meetings, conversations, memos, letters — most business things — in exactly this way. Put two focused businesspeople on a beach together and, unless they are in a leisure mode (which won't last for long), they'll get right to it.

goal	Wanna dig a hole?
obstacle	Sure. We need a shovel.
resource	No, let's just use our hands.
obstacle	I have a cut on my hand.
plan	Okay, we need to get you a little shovel and I'll use my hands.
resource	Hey, that kid over there has a shovel.
plan	Let's get it.
obstacle	No, his mother's right next to him, she might make a fuss.
plan	Let's bribe the kid.
plan	Yeah, we'll trade for it. What do we have to trade?
resource	I've got 50 cents here.
obstacle	The shovel's not even worth that much! (efficiency issue)
plan	How about we just ask if we can borrow it? Good idea. (positive reinforcement — empathy gesture)
implement	Hi, young fella. Do you mind if we borrow your shovel? We just want it for a couple of minutes. Please?
goal	Great. Okay, how deep do we dig?
obstacle	I don't know. Why are we digging?
goal	For fun. Oh, never mind. (not a fulfilling goal)

When goals are sincerely held, they motivate. In fact, when someone announces that they have a goal, they are implicitly acknowledging that they want, at some level at least, to reach it. And focused business-people on the job are always reaching.

Are you reaching? Do your employees all have goals? Are they working towards them efficiently? Is the team you are responsible for driving towards a clearly defined goal? Is it doing an efficient job? Are your conversations goal-directed? Are they direct? If not, what's holding you back? Removing that obstacle is the key to reaching the goal of having goals and efficiently pursuing them.

FULFILLING GOALS

Highly focused people not only think in terms of goals, they also tend to fulfill them. Many managers I know are good at following the agenda described in this chapter but they tend to fall down on the completion side. This is an unusually common weakness. It is almost as though they focus on goals but they lose their concentration.

I call this problem "forgetting conviction." Often people announce to the world with great conviction that they are going to do some good thing — quit smoking, lose weight, exercise, hit some target down the road; in other words, meet a goal that takes some degree of concentration over a prolonged period — and then ultimately never come through. When they make their announcement they have two things going for them: the intention to act and the conviction to act. After a while, though, they seem to forget the conviction. They remember the intention — that's an intellectual thing — but they no longer have that teeth-gritting, fist-clenching verve. They wander off track. They lose their focus. They have the rational agenda down clearly, but they are weak on implementation.

When you manage people like this, one of the solutions is for you to develop the skill of "closing loops." When someone commits to a task, and they fully intend to act and they have the sincere conviction, but not the capacity to go all the way, if you just say, "Okay, go for it," they won't come through. In order to keep them on track you need to hold them accountable, to take some step to remind them of, or renew, their conviction. So you install a system to make sure that you find out how they are doing. You don't ask them to keep you informed — that wouldn't truly be closing the loop because there is no guarantee that they will remember or be inclined to report in. Indeed, you need some way to minimize the chance that implementation will simply die out.

One easy way is to file commitments people make in some personal carry-forward system. Sometimes when someone commits to me that they will do a certain thing by a certain day, I record in my calendar that I can expect to see it on that day. If I don't see it, I am reminded by the note in my calendar. If I do see what was promised to me, everything is great.

Highly focused managers have loop closing down to a habit. They don't assume that everyone will necessarily come through. They make private notes to keep tasks under control. On the other hand, they also don't offend people by making the little notes a sign of mistrust. It's a discreet process. But over time employees begin to realize that commitments mean commitments and they learn to hold themselves accountable — they do what they say they will do.

WHEN MANAGERS DON'T FOCUS

If you as manager are not particularly effective at following through on commitments made to yourself, let alone those made to you by others, then you have a focusing problem. You can close loops for yourself, but you are also prone to forgive yourself. When your lovely time management system alerts you to what you intended to do, you might forgive yourself for not acting and carry forward the reminder to some later date. Closing the loops for others makes them accountable. After all, you are the boss. We all know that you have the secret leverage. Closing loops on yourself does not have the same guarantee.

This is a tough problem to overcome. Committing to your own boss can help. Announcing your intentions to your employees can help, but involves the risk of embarrassment and bad role modelling should you fail to deliver. I had a client who owned his own business and who had a big problem with this. He was a highly logical, rational man. He had that aspect of focus down to a science. The problem was that he had this amazing reputation, even in his own organization, of promising things and not delivering. Needless to say, this was very damaging. He had a hundred employees and all of them knew his reputation, and it had a major effect on their own tendency to fulfill commitments — they didn't.

The client's problem was that he had great ideas, a logical approach, tremendous people skills, but terrible long-term concentration. And he couldn't sustain his focus. He had no one to hold him accountable — except me. We made a deal. I would manage him.

What leverage did I have? He gave me a written agreement that every time he did not fulfill a commitment made to me, I could fine him. Monthly fines could not exceed $5,000.

We met weekly. I would manage him during these meetings, just like I would manage my own team. I would uncover his goals, ask for his plans, nail down dates by which he would have things done, help him work through obstacles, help him develop and revise his plans, and record his commitments. The next week, if he didn't come through, I would levy the fine.

After about three months of $5,000 in fines, two interesting things happened. One was that he developed the habit of coming through. We essentially trained his brain to sustain concentration. This, I suppose, is the effect of closing loops with people: they learn to come through. The second effect was that he stopped making grandiose commitments. He stayed realistic in his promises so that he would avoid the fine.

None of this is to say that you have to fine people to instill in them a follow-through mentality. But you do need a method of tactfully making people understand that you are serious about coming through. If you say to a person who promises to do a certain thing by the end of the month that you look forward to seeing at the end of the month how it goes, and you write down in your book that you can expect it, and then at the end of the month it's still not done, you can't just drop it. And you can't be a meanie about it either. You need an empathetic way of pursuing it — relentlessly.

This leads us to what I would call my description of

the best way to manage: be a really warm, really open, really friendly, nit-picky SOB.

Really warm means you care and you are compassionate. You are authentic in your caring about people.

Really open means that you share whatever can be shared. You are more open than closed. Certainly there are things that cannot be shared — we all know what they are: plans to close down, security issues, private matters about other people — but generally, you are open about your thoughts, feelings, and concerns.

Really friendly means you create an enjoyable environment. You say your warm hellos, you say good-bye at the end of the day, you share appropriate humour, you spend chat time with people, you make it a point to be friendly with all.

Nit-picky means that all things matter around here. We are on a quest to be perfect. Minute details matter. You role-model it. You expect it. You applaud attention to detail. Details are royalty. Details make the difference.

The SOB part means that your quest for commitment fulfillment, for detail-orientation, for tidiness and order is relentless. The SOB part means you send the message, "Let's not pretend that it's okay not to do what we say we are going to do." You won't stop. You just won't stop. Victim thinking is not allowed. Agents are rewarded.

How does the SOB stuff show up when somebody lets you down? Nicely. In fact, my favourite way of dealing with someone on my team who frequently lets me down is to say something like what is in the paragraph below. This effort is not something you use regularly; it's a last resort. But it is very effective.

I don't get it. You committed to doing this and you didn't keep your commitment. Of course, this has happened to us before. And I'm not exactly sure what you think I should be doing about it. For me, these commitments you make matter. I don't get it. What should I do when this happens? When you promise to do something and then you don't keep your promise, what should I do? Seriously, what should I do?

Then you stay quiet. If there is a long silence, you ask again. But you ask sincerely. Never propose a punishment. Let them do it. Send them home to think about it, if necessary. Usually it doesn't go so far that people say, "If I do it again, you can fire me." It usually stops with some form of awkward humour from the employee. Let them bring up the humour. Sometimes it finishes with a realistic punishment. Yet the real negative reinforcement occurs not in the subsequent punishment but in the intensity of the interaction. People are not accustomed to it.

It is not a game. It is one human asking another human about commitments. The legitimacy of the question rests in the authenticity of human interaction. There is an implicit agreement between people that we fulfill commitments. If we all went around not fulfilling commitments, our society would collapse. A rule in Kantian ethics called the categorical imperative says that for that reason breaking commitments is immoral. All you are doing with this line of questioning is dealing with reality. I wouldn't call it hard ball. I wouldn't call it soft ball. I call it real ball.

So focus means being rational in your approach

to goals and it means staying on track. It means keeping other people on track. It means being willing to confront.

LINKAGE

If focus is balanced with empathy, then a tremendous management potential arises. It is the potential to "link." Linkage is a key business skill. If you can link your goals to a customer's goals, and you can make and implement effective plans, you have the formula for success. The same principle applies to coaching people. If you can link what you want out of people with what they want out of their job, you have what it takes to motivate. This is the heart of coaching, which we will look at closely in the next chapter.

For example, if an employee wants to be wealthy and you want to sell more, the linkage lies in selling more for you in order to find greater wealth for him. If an employee wants to get a promotion and you want her to stop spitting at customers, the link is obvious: "Stop spitting and you have a better chance of getting promoted."

Salespeople who have a consultative style seek to create linkage for a living. They ask questions to uncover customer needs and opportunities. They see the link between these needs and what they have to offer, and then they pitch their products and services, described in a way that shows the customer how the customer's goals are fulfilled by buying from that salesperson. The salesperson who recognizes links and describes them the most clearly is likely to be the most successful.

Linkage is a big thing. It is one of the values derived from blending focus and empathy. We don't just press, press, press. We press and we release. There is a rhythm to it.

COACHING NINE

Coaching is one of the key responsibilities of leaders or managers — conducting formal and informal conversations to help people be more effective on the job. Very few managers take enough time to do it. Most of us fall into the rut of simply managing the day-to-day functions.

It's a shame because, not only is it our job, it helps us to fulfill our management mandate more effectively if we are leading people who are constantly getting better and better. We also derive moral benefit: we have a valuable perspective to offer and it is inherently good to offer it. It even makes us more promotable, because our area of responsibility — our department or organization — performs better, and because we have prepared people to assume more responsibility.

In fact, developing people is critical to a rational approach to business management. We have a goal to reach or a vision to fulfill, so presumably we are not there yet and we want to be. If we want to reach this goal, then we are constantly implementing plans to overcome the internal and external obstacles to doing so. Optimal people performance improves the probability and speed of our team fulfilling its vision; it helps us overcome the obstacle presented by people not working at their best — so it is rational to optimize their performance. Coaching makes sense.

WHY DON'T MANAGERS COACH?

There are many reasons managers don't coach their employees. We lack the time, for example. This is a very busy age, often with more to do than can be done. Many managers allege that they don't have the time to groom their people. A counter to this point, however, is that we can save time by developing our people. When they get better at their jobs, we can afford to do fewer of the things we had been doing before and can attend to higher-level tasks such as thinking and planning. The time complaint is a manifestation of the old urgent versus important battle — there are so many urgent things to do that we don't have time to do the important ones. But if we force ourselves to take the correct time to do the important things, we can reduce the number of urgent matters that arise and we can be safer in delegating the urgent things.

I'm a great believer in managers working towards a private goal of not doing anything but thinking, planning, coaching people, assigning tasks, and signing letters and other documents. I have had many clients claim that they don't want the supervisors aspiring to this goal because they think frontline leaders should be doers, not thinkers. But I have never been convinced of this. Teams can go much further when there is somebody steering the ship, somebody who is up there in the wheelhouse who can see the big picture. My more flexible clients who resisted the idea of supervisors preparing everybody under them to do all things, and who let me assist in the conversion of "doer" supervisors into pure "thinking" leaders, have all seen the conversion work. Whether it is in a simple retail environment or on the factory floor, full delegation can be very effective. The full-time job of the supervisor includes a major focus on developing people to do what was formerly done by the boss.

Another common reason managers don't do enough coaching is that they are uncomfortable with the process. They correctly perceive that to coach means to define where somebody needs to get better and to point out the desired correction. It's the pointing-it-out that they don't want to do, usually because they fear confrontation. Who wants to deal with the defensiveness and argument involved in criticizing somebody? Yet by creating an environment where people see coaching as a given and by adopting effective tools for criticism, much of the painful part of coaching can be eliminated.

An additional reason that managers don't coach is that they think the employees are already good enough, that the team is functioning pretty nicely already. Why mess with a good thing? The thinking here is that even though the organization may not have met its goals, the managers don't perceive that improving employee performance will sufficiently improve the chances of attaining the desired goals. This reasoning misses a fundamental principle behind the operation of our society: the need to better ourselves continually (an idea I deal with in depth in the next chapter). It is smart to assume that we don't want to stop getting better. There's the competition to worry about, the rationalization of cost centres, the potential boredom of the team, the growing expectations of customers, maybe even the nature of life itself — growth and evolution need to be encouraged.

Sometimes managers don't coach because they don't know the job of the person they have to coach. But here's a piece of good news: you don't have to know much about a job to coach someone to do it better. First of all, you can always ask the employee, and you'll most likely get an answer because most people know how they could be better at their jobs. In fact, if you know the desired output of a function, you and the employee can brainstorm the methods of improving it. Improvement usually comes in quantity, efficiency, and quality. By talking about these three aims, you can usually find methods for improvement.

And then there is the individual. If the job is really being done to optimum satisfaction levels, we still have the challenge of the job satisfaction of the employee. This too falls into the realm of the coach. We coach not just to get improved performance but to help people find fulfillment as well. We can ask, "What would make you happier?" Or, in response to those alleging happiness, "What would make you even happier?" It never has to stop.

Not long ago, I could not juggle three little sandbags in the air. But I coached someone else who was unable to juggle, and I helped that person to learn how. Simply by knowing that juggling requires a person to keep his elbows in and his eyes staring at a certain spot, I was able to provide feedback to him — feedback that he couldn't get from himself — and watch his skills evolve. You don't have to know how to do something in order to help someone do it better.

WHAT IS COACHING?

Enough about why people don't coach. Let's discuss what coaching actually is. Coaching is the process of providing feedback to people that, when coupled with their own thoughts, helps them to do something better. It involves creating an environment where they are open to the feedback. It involves getting a commitment to make the agreed-upon change. It ultimately involves assessing the success of the change in order to give more feedback. It is about goals, and doing things differently over time in order to attain those goals.

Sometimes we give input on the fly, when we spend little time but make suggestions that we believe will help. This is not coaching. On-the-fly input is one-way communication, rather than two-way. And it is very informal.

We need to be nice about on-the-fly delivery. It can be offensive if delivered without regard for the feelings of the person being coached. Style makes a big difference here. Yelling out "I told you to rinse the dishes before you dry them!" is not nearly as nice to hear as "You know, soap affects the flavour of food, so it would be good if you could rinse before you dry."

Tone of voice can influence on-the-fly feedback. Say the following sentence ten times, and each time put the emphasis on a different word: "I thought I told you to please rinse the dishes." For example, the first time, the emphasis belongs on the first "I." In the second, place the emphasis on the word "thought," and so on. Notice how inflection changes the message being sent. Some placements of inflection sound arrogant. At least one sounds humble. Anger gets projected in another.

125

Facial expressions can also affect what is being said. Delivery with a smile can be much more effective than delivery with a scowl. Try videotaping yourself in a role-play context. You may be surprised at your image and your tone too.

You may be thinking, "Oh, come on! You mean I need to watch my everyday communication style? Give me a break! Surely I can be myself on the job!" Well, perhaps not quite. Many of us do not know how we appear to others. I know many managers who are unaware of their aggressive communication style. They have no inkling of how they hurt the feelings of the people on their teams. Their employees tell consultants like me about it because they have no idea how to communicate to the boss about it. I am not even remotely suggesting that you watch your style at home or otherwise away from work — that's your business, of course — but on the job, most moments matter. Goals, at some level, are clear. We need to employ the method that optimizes our chance of attaining goals effectively and efficiently. It's a job, this management thing.

But as I said, giving input on the fly is not coaching. And nor is coaching about job reviews, those annual events where managers dump all over their people the things they save up in a drawer because, for all sorts of reasons, they didn't address the problems when they occurred. Rather, coaching is about communicating, every day, in a two-way conversation about reaching goals.

COACHING GUIDELINES

Some guidelines are in order. First, we need empathy. It is important to see the world view of the person you are coaching in order to optimize the extent to which they hear your input. This is a press and release process. Press, press, press just builds resentment and no change will be adopted.

It is just as important to support the self-esteem of the person we are coaching by providing positive observation during a coaching conversation. For example, if, right after a conversation we overheard with a customer, we were coaching a salesperson about speaking too quickly, we might say,

> Linda you did a great job listing all of the benefits the way you did, and I like the rapport you built with the person; she's not the kind of person it is easy to warm up to and you did it well. My only criticism would be that you talked fairly quickly, so it made it hard to follow everything you said. What do you think about your speed?

Notice how Linda's self-esteem is supported by the initial comments about her benefit-selling and rapport-building efforts. In the same way that empathy stops chatter because a person hears their thoughts in the speech of the other, positive comments grab a person's attention because they reinforce the person's self-worth.

Also notice how the points were in reference to a goal; in this case the goal was "to follow what was said."

Notice, too how the comments ended with a question. This is not destined to be a one-way conversation. We try to involve the person in the conversation as much as possible. Coaching is not a press, press, press event. It is an interaction. In fact, our questions are ideal if they are the type that encourage more than a one-word answer — if they are, in essence, open probes aimed at encouraging greater involvement.

If used incorrectly, closed probes, those soliciting a one-word response — "yes," "no," "six" — can turn a coaching interaction into a manipulative interrogation. Don't copy the style below; it's much too aggressive.

Coach: Did you feel you were going too fast?
Teammate: Maybe a little.
Coach: You don't want to go too fast, do you?
Teammate: No.
Coach: Because if you go too fast, people can't understand what you are saying, can they?
Teammate: No.
Coach: And then you won't get communication, will you?
Teammate: No.
Coach: Good. I'm glad we sorted that out.

Aside from making the person being coached feel coerced into compliance, closed probes rob the coach of valuable opinions that might enhance the quality of the conversation. You want the people on your team to feel good about your coaching conversations. By openly including them and by making them feel valuable, you maximize your chances of doing so.

Employee involvement is not the only way to make people receptive to your input. It is important to create the right culture among the group you lead, a culture wherein developmental conversations occur regularly. The best managers I know make it clear to all their employees that one of the most important parts of the management role is to groom people for more responsibilities. In this context, employees recognize that when you are in a coaching mode, you are just doing your job.

ADOPTING A COACHING CULTURE

For managers who have not been in the habit of coaching but who want to start, there are things you can say to prepare your team for your new modus operandi. For example,

> I have been thinking lately that I am somewhat stuck in my job, because I have not groomed people to handle more responsibility. So I am embarking on a major task to make me more dispensable. This is the only way I am going to get promoted. So I want to change the nature of our relationship and begin preparing you to handle more than you do now. This doesn't mean I am promising you my job when I move on. In fact, I am going to go through this process with everyone on the team. But I am going to stretch everyone a bit. I want to steer people only in the directions they want to go, so it should be good news for all.

Or,

> I have decided that I have sort of let you all down by not spending enough time developing you for the future. We are so busy around here that people development is not something we

have done a lot of. The team has suffered; you have suffered personally and I have not done my job. I want to announce that I am committed to spending time helping you to define and reach your career goals. Between your insights about where you want to go and what changes you need to make to get there and my own thoughts about how you might develop, I think we can make this new direction valuable for all. The organization will win because it will employ more-qualified people. I will win by being able to entrust more responsibility. And you will win because you will be better equipped to do what you want to do.

If you couple these statements with other components of an effective vision, such as anticipating your audience's chatter on the matter and how you expect they will have to stretch in order to grow, you will be able to begin a shift to a coaching culture. Just be sure that once you start, you stay on course.

THE COACHING CONVERSATION

Now that we have a few guidelines to follow, let's consider the coaching agenda, the steps to take before and during the coaching conversation. By following the sequence outlined here, you will be able to conduct coaching conversations that inspire, bring value, lead to change, and help you fulfill your mandate and reach your and your team's goals.

Before a coaching conversation can begin, you have to define, in a preliminary way, the criticism you wish to levy. I say "preliminary" because once your conversation begins, you may have to wander off course a bit to pursue an unanticipated matter that arises in the conversation. You may start a talk with the intention of telling a manager that you don't think she coaches her team frequently enough, only to be taken off course when this person replies that her biggest weakness is in managing time. To avoid burdening this person with more negatives, you can place your own agenda on the back burner and spend your time on her organizational skills instead.

To determine the criticism you want to raise, you might undertake what is referred to as a "gap analysis." This is where you define an ideal and compare it to the present, in order to see the obvious gap, or change, required to fulfill the ideal. Let's say you manage a manager. You ask yourself, "What would this guy be like or what would he be doing if I was totally satisfied with his performance?" You list the traits he would possess or the tasks he would be undertaking. (Sometimes a person's job description will tell you this.) Then you assess or score him in those areas. On the important matters, where the score is low, you would call that a coaching opportunity, or "pinch point," indicating the criticism you want to levy.

Sometimes, you will get a long list of pinch points; sometimes you will get a short one. Choose the one that you would like to address in your next coaching conversation. It is valuable to sort out in your mind how you want to communicate the pinch point.

REVISITING META-LEVELS

In chapter 5 we discussed using meta-levels to help you make your concerns about employee attitudes clear. We saw that a meta-level is a way to communicate the big picture to an employee in such a way that it allows the employee to see herself. Rather than just citing your concern, you couch it in a broader context. For example, if someone on your team tends to be late completing assignments, rather than saying, "You were late on that assignment and that was a problem," you might say, "Over the past two months, you have agreed to do several things by a certain time and in many cases you did not get them done by the promised deadline."

The other way we described using meta-levels was to place the concern under a broader umbrella or category. For example, rather than referring to a missed deadline, we might refer to the broader notion of keeping promises. Broader still might be the notion of professionalism. So we could say, "In the context of your professional development, I think we should look at . . ." Again, meta-level communication tends to centre the listener and improves his receiving the desired message.

Another way to place a concern into a meta-level context involves referring to the here and now. It too tends to take the specific concern and put it into a context that enables understanding. For example, "I'm feeling really frustrated right now about the fact that you said you would get this thing done by now and it is not done." To employ some empathy, we could add, "You may be thinking that I'm going overboard about this since it seems so small, but . . ."

Still another use of meta-levels is to refer to cause and effect. When people see how what they have done (or not done) has a consequence, they take their attention off the single point and put it into a broader context. "By being late with this thing you are holding up a series of other steps that need to be taken." Again, we are helping the person to step back from the idea of the single indiscretion and see the big picture.

The final meta-level tool to be discussed here (although there are many other possibilities) concerns one of the thrusts of this whole book: shared goals. If we can link our goal for the employee to the employee's goals, then we can once again take attention away from a single occurrence and broaden it in a way that helps the employee see the matter in a bigger context. For example, "We have discussed your desire to move past this job and it makes sense that your ability to get things done on time is a prerequisite for doing so."

This last approach needs to be used in almost all coaching conversations. It is one that can be combined with at least one of the others. Since you want to add value to the person, you also want the conversation to be two-sided. That is, not only do you think of what change it would be good for you to see in this person, you have to make sure that the change would be good for the person as well. In other words, you want to anticipate her goal. If the person's goal is to get promoted, then that is relevant to the coaching. You must link what you want out of the person with what she wants for herself. This is the hard part about coaching.

We are back to linkage here — back to the balance between focus and empathy. If you were all focus, all press, then you would coach people only on the changes you wanted them to make, with no regard for what they wanted out of their job. But this would not be good. We want a balance between your goals (self) and their goals (other). We don't want compromise — that's not the right kind of balance. We want collaboration. We want both parties to win in the process. We want to link our goal for the conversation with one of their goals.

It is much easier to do this if you have balanced levels of empathy and focus. If you have lots of focus, then where you want to go in the conversation is clear. If you have lots of empathy, then you know where the other person wants to go. Linking these is the key skill of management.

Of course, one of the advantages of finding the link is that you virtually guarantee yourself that the person will be motivated to make the desired changes. If you do not find the link, then their chatter during the critical conversation will not support you and will prevent you from being fully heard.

Let's say you want to coach a manager to spend more time coaching his own people. You arrived at the goal for the conversation through a gap analysis. You said to yourself that your goal for that role is for the manager to be a people developer. Then you concluded that this particular manager did not groom his people. You concluded that your goal for the next coaching conversation was to raise the matter of his being more focused on people development. That he wasn't doing it enough was your pinch point. That it is good for the organization to develop people because the competition is doing it may be the meta-level description. Then you do the next step: you ask yourself, "What, as far as I know, does this manager want?" You might answer, "I'm pretty sure this guy wants my job." Then comes the magical link. In this case, it is a fairly simple one. You conclude that you want to tie his ability to get your job at least partially to his getting better at developing people.

In this way, linkage becomes the kind of meta-level context we have discussed. We are saying to our manager, to get what you want, you need to develop your people. He then sees developing people in a bigger context. Another meta-level description would say, "Fred said you didn't develop him. I venture to suggest that there may be a pattern here." Yet another meta-level delivery would involve saying, "The competition is killing us and we need to do everything we possibly can to give us an edge. One of the things I'd like you to focus on is the one-on-one development of your people." The least potent way to levy the criticism, a way where no meta-level would be employed, is to simply say: "Develop your people."

Linkage is sometimes easy, sometimes difficult. After all, in some environments people don't seem to have many goals. Take some union situations, for example. There are many people who don't appear to be open to management input, let alone being open to a developmental conversation with their manager, without a shop steward present. And sometimes employees in these circumstances actually shut themselves off from thinking about goals. On the other hand, I have seen tough union situations where coaching towards employee goals works the vast majority of the time. The employee goals may just be to avoid having to do a job again and again, or to avoid having to walk half a mile for a part, or to keep the boss off his back, or to perform the job as well as it can be performed — there are usually goals in there if we look hard enough.

Sometimes we just have to ask, "What makes a good day for you?" Or, "What's your biggest challenge?" Or, "What bugs you about your job?" The answers reveal employee goals. Linkage possibilities follow.

So, you have the pinch point, you have anticipated the employee's goal, and you have the link prepared. It's time to start the conversation. All the planning, however, doesn't preclude digression. You have to be prepared to go elsewhere once talk starts up. Either the employee goal will be different from what you predicted or you will decide that it is not the right time to raise your pinch point. You have to be prepared to change your plans as you go. It's challenging, but it is better than starting a coaching conversation without a plan of any kind.

COACHING STEPS

The steps of coaching are straightforward. First, we raise the employee's goal in conversation. Then we communicate the pinch point, in a meta-level context. We proceed to discuss and agree on the desired change. Finally, we close the loop by creating a plan in a way that ensures change will really occur.

We can bring up the topic of the employee's goal slowly or directly. Here are some examples.

- I'd like to talk with you about what we do when customers approach the counter. Tell me, what is our goal each time this occurs?
- Let's talk about how you repaired that equipment. What was your goal?
- I'd like to talk with you about how you're doing with that report. My impression is that the goal is to sell them on moving forward, is that right?
- I'd like to talk with you about your long-term plans concerning the XYZ development. What's the goal here?
- I'd like to talk with you about your long-term career plans. Where do you want to go?
- I'd like to talk with you about morale in the office. Obviously we want to make it better. Do you have any thoughts about this?
- I'd like to talk with you about our error rate in the back production. I'd like to reduce it. What is a reasonable goal to set?

Once the employee's goal has been raised in the conversation, you are in a position to link the change you wish to how the employee can reach his goal. Let's use the example again of your coaching a manager to do more coaching with his people. Assume you expect his goal is to get your job. Notice how, in this example, the coach raises the pinch point in a very roundabout fashion.

> *Coach:* I'd like to talk with you about our strategies to deal with the mounting competitive pressures. The conclusion we reached at the last directors' meeting was that we need to focus much more on training and developing our people. What are your thoughts about that?

137

Coachee: It's impossible to find the time for any one-on-ones around here. But I'm very open to bringing in the Human Resources folks for a few training sessions.

Coach: Good idea. What else can we do?

Coachee: I haven't thought much about it. What do you think?

Coach: Well, I agree that one of our weak spots is our people. We don't pay them as much as the competition. We don't train them as much either. And frankly, we're not so hot at succession planning. My impression is that you and a few of your colleagues want my job and I'm not spending enough time grooming or challenging you. My bet is that you are in the same boat. Is that right?

Coachee: That I want your job? You bet. And it's probably true that I'm not delegating enough.

Coach: Delegating is one means, but we need to make a deliberate thing out of one-on-one coaching. You said it's hard to find the time; how much time have you been spending on one-on-ones?

Coachee: About zero minutes per month.

Coach: Right. Do you agree you need to do it a lot? And that lacking time won't cut it as an explanation for not doing it?

Coachee: I suppose, but I don't know where I'm going to find the time.

Coach: Then I guess you need to plan for it. I think it's safe to assume it's a must. So it probably needs an official time allocation. I guess I'd like to see two things: a plan that shows how much time you will put into one-on-ones and also a fairly detailed development plan for each of your people. That way, we can begin to deal with the personnel side of the competitive issue fairly logically and we can both get started on succession planning. Are you okay with that?

Coachee: Sure.

Coach: When do you think I can see something in writing? It can be informal, but I do want to do this thoroughly. We're talking about a fairly big venture here. And sooner is better than later.

The coach raised the desired matter very indirectly. The topic of coaching arose. The pinch point was delivered gently. The desired change was linked to the goals of the person being coached. On the other hand, no promises were made. An unexpected objection arose — that there was no time. But the coach followed a valuable rule of thumb: when in doubt, ask for a plan. A commitment to act was solicited and an effort to close the loop was made successfully.

Here's another example. In this case, the coach is a human resources supervisor chatting with a new employee who doesn't seem to understand that Human Resources (HR) serves internal customers and that the internal customers must feel well served.

Coach: Linda, how's it going?

Coachee: Great. I love the job.

Coach: I think it's time for me to add one more nugget to the things you need to think

about it. Are you familiar with the concept
of internal customers?

Coachee: Sure. It's everybody we serve, right? All
the employees of the company. Yeah, I
understand that. Why, is there some
problem?

Coach: No. But there is something new to add to
your bag of tricks. Tell me, what do you
think are our goals here in HR?

Coachee: I guess to get people the information they
want. To be really accurate. To help people.

Coach: Right. Excellent. I know you want to do a
great job. I can tell. So, there's one more to
add to the list. Not only do we want to do
what you just said, we also want to make
the people we serve *feel* that we are serving
them well. It's on top of everything you
named. Do you know what I mean?

Coachee: I think so.

Coach: What are some things we can do to make
people recognize how well we serve them,
aside from getting them the information
they need?

Coachee: I don't know.

Coach: Well, we can go out of our way to be polite.
For example, when Mr. Jones was standing
over by the printer waiting for you to get
off the phone, you could have shown some
sign that you knew he was there. And when
you put someone on hold, you could pick up
the phone every half minute to tell them that
you are still working on the matter.
What else can you think of?

Coachee: Well, I suppose saying please and thank you would be smart.

Coach: Great. What else?

Coachee: Getting back to people even if you don't have an answer was something they taught us in customer service in my last job.

Coach: Perfect. You've got it. Now please don't get the impression that I'm in any way unhappy with what you have done. I just wanted to add to your training. Let's both keep an eye on this habit, and I do think it is a habit we all have to develop, and make a point of talking about it again next week — let's say Thursday after the meeting. What do you say?

Coachee: Sounds good. I'll watch how I do and I'd appreciate you watching me. I really do want to do well.

Coach: I know you do, and I'm going to do everything I can to help you.

Many notable things occurred in this coaching inter-action. First, notice how the guidelines were met. The coach supported the self-esteem of the employee by using words like "right" and "excellent." The coach also said that no problem was being addressed in this conversation; her message was positioned as a simple next step in the employee's development. She essentially said, "Don't think I'm not happy with your performance." She was simply adding to the list of good things to do. Also, the coach showed an understanding of the new employee's straightforward goal — to be great at her job — and she tactfully linked her message to that goal.

I hope you can see that coaching is a non-threatening activity that can help you fulfill your own goals and assist you in helping your employees fulfill their own goals. It's a press and release process that challenges your linking skills. It is not easy. But it is very important.

THE BALANCING ACT

IT is said that when we are born, we are dependent. By teenage years, we become independent. Later, we develop sensibilities that are labelled codependent. Finally, when fully mature, humans find interdependence. At this last stage in our development we recognize the interdependence of people, and even the interdependence between people and the surrounding world. We achieve a kind of global world view where linkage is seen in all that we do.

I propose to you that this is the world view of the mature manager or leader. The goals of the organization, the goals of the individuals being led, the goals of the customers being served, and the well-being of society are all being supported.

Self-centred managers can't manifest this global perspective. They are too interested in fulfilling what might be termed their short-sighted goals. Only by opening up to the needs and perspectives of others can one find the required linkage. As we said before, allowing the perspectives of others to enter the picture seems risky to press-press-press individuals. They naturally fear that by taking the risk, they forfeit what they seek. In the same way that children want what they want when they want it, and cannot understand the value of some healthy self-denial, self-oriented individuals deny themselves the chance to gain the respect of others that they so dearly seek.

One of the biggest keys to leadership rests in this ironic trait of nature. If you demand respect from those you lead, then they will deny you what you seek. If you are recognized as willing to go without the respect, focusing instead on the task at hand, they will tend to grant respect to you. There are several reasons for this.

RECIPROCITY

My favourite explanation comes from the principle of reciprocity — a well-studied human tendency to feel indebted to those who do favours for us. Reciprocity says that if you do something for me, then I will likely feel that I owe you something in return.

Reciprocity is responsible for whole industries. For example, the advertising specialty industry — ad spec — is premised on our feelings of indebtedness to those who give us freebies. It's in the business of producing hand-out refrigerator magnets, coffee cups with corporate logos splashed across the sides, and pens with the donor's name printed on them, all with the goal of engendering an unconscious commitment to return the favour. Reciprocity is also at the heart of customer service. When we take profoundly good care of our customers, they feel obliged, for a while, to stick with us. When we offer good value to our customers, they keep buying from us. We really can earn favour.

Leadership works in the same way. If a leader is nice to an employee, the employee will return the favour and be nice back. If a leader goes beyond simply being nice, and offers value or benefit to the employee, then the employee will tend to go out of her way to offer value to the whole organization.

If you don't engage reciprocity, then you engage the reverse. This is a common phenomenon for overly aggressive managers. When the manager gets tough, the employees jump all right, but their self-talk mutters: "I'll get you back in my own little way."

At play here is what social psychologists refer to as psychological reactance, or reverse reciprocity. It is the same principle that makes the terrible twos so terrible, makes teenagers rebel, and is what Shakespeare played out in *Romeo and Juliet*. The more the two lovers were denied the freedom to have each other, the stronger their love became. If you deny people their freedom, they kick their feet. But if you grant them the freedom, they stay. There is a reason that the old dictum "If you love someone, set them free" works.

I know a manager who is about as far from humble as one can get. He justifies his self-confidence by attributing it to dynamism. He cites dynamism as a key leadership trait. He walks into his facility and loudly declares, "Hello, everyone!" then he'll throw in some humour: "I bet you've been waiting for the big guy to show up, haven't you? Hey, Lisa, do you like my tie? I think it suits me, don't you?" Then he laughs as the folks in the office chuckle and roll their eyes. They're struck by his arrogance; he's laughing because of the attention he's won. And another day begins.

Do they feel led by an effective leader? Do they feel heard? The answer, of course, is a resounding no. They resent being nobodies in the boss's private world.

There is a lightness in the office, though. Chuckles abound. But people are not fulfilled. There is a oneness in the team (they are unified in their incredulity and hostility), but people don't really like working for the man. They get lost in his shadow.

BLENDING MOTIVES

We have our dualism showing here, if you can spot it. Press, press, press and people will resent, resent, resent. Pure release, on the other hand, doesn't work either, because people want leadership. We must blend these two motives. It's a balancing act.

But do we balance by being self-oriented at one moment and other-oriented in the next? Or do we somehow blend the two motives into one stream of consciousness? My opinion is that we tend to alternate moments when we are new at the game. And then, as we evolve, and get better at finding linkage, we discover the formula for blending. It starts with vacillation. Then we get into the same sort of "zone" looked at in chapter 5, where we attend to both directions at once.

From that bird's-eye zone, that meta-level visionary place, the mature manager can bring value to many. And each of us — employees, employers, customers, society, the planet itself — wants value. This is not the notion of value for money, as in assessing a bottle of wine or getting a fair price for one's dollar. It refers to goal fulfillment. It refers to problem solving; to making life easier, making it better, bringing pleasure, reducing pain, saving time. It refers to pleasant surprises, helping in times of need, satisfying curiosity, uncovering opportunity, helping people get to where they want to be, sorting things out, overcoming obstacles, reducing risk, improving efficiency, making more money, bringing laughter, tidying up — whatever makes us happy, long term and short term.

I know a manager who was approached by an employee for more money. His response was simple: bring greater value and I will gladly pay more; actually cause the organization to derive extra benefit in some way, and suddenly you will be worth more. His message asked: "Why would I want to pay more without getting more in return. We both agreed that what you were earning was fair, so what's different — your seniority?" He has what may be a valid point in his press response.

I have personally been flattered with a request for a simple answer to the question "What is the key to business?" Forced to be brief, my answer comes in three words: Just bring value. Bring value and they will buy. Isn't that what product differentiation is all about? Isn't that what finding employment is all about? Surely it is at the heart of selling. When the perceived value of what you bring to the table is greater than the perceived value that is offered by others, customers will buy from you. When it is not, then they will not. In sales, the trick is to find out what value they seek.

I have seen a lot of companies wrestle with problems caused by competitive pressure, where salespeople say, "We have to lower our prices to survive. The competition is deadly." I've been in boardrooms where senior leaders sit pondering how they can cut their costs in order to become more efficient so they can cope with pressures on pricing. I've seen huge brandname organizations struggle with the fact that no-name products are stealing their market share and the brand people exclaim, "Our brand is losing its value, we have to promote the brand! We have to teach the sales force to sell the brand! Otherwise, we're doomed!"

I propose the solution to these dilemmas is clear — difficult to achieve, perhaps, but clear. Just bring value. Don't cut costs, innovate! Don't cut prices, innovate! Do something smart, and earn your salary! That's what the founder of your organization did. That's why you made it to management. Now the game is getting tough, and you are being challenged. Will you lie down and die or will you meet the challenge? Finding that zone where empathy and focus are in balance, where we can simultaneously see the value others seek while still being in touch with our own goals, helps us meet the challenge.

Business operates in stages. Somebody comes up with a neat idea. Value. They make money offering this value to the market. All is well. Then other people see the money being made and they want it too. They compete. Nature begins to take its course. Somebody makes their competitive product better. Somebody else does it cheaper. Everybody is finding a little niche. Other people crawl into the same niche. Pressures mount. And then, everybody is close to being the same. They get into the game called "value added." They start throwing things in for free, nice little gestures that often truly do help to differentiate them for a while — until other folks offer the same value added and the gesture gets taken for granted by the customers. Then what was once added value no longer qualifies as value added. Everybody starts looking for new value added. They declare things are value added when, in fact, they really don't offer extra value. And people sit around boardrooms sweating. "What are we going to do?" And I say, bring value and they will buy.

Innovate! The survival instinct is so deeply ingrained, so purely self-oriented, that the hunger to survive denies the survival. The solution can't be press, press, press. No, we have to become focused on things outside our little world views in order to discover what value people seek. Creativity comes from breaking out of the box, not from looking inside it.

Easier said than done. Sometimes I think that only geniuses can pull it off. Only certain people have what it takes to generate the special idea. Huge brand corporations, when their name alone doesn't represent distinct value, face a real adult problem. They often have the greatest minds around working in their organizations. I think the last thing they should do is cut. They have to break out of the box. They usually have to do it fast, because infrastructure is like a monster that keeps eating resources. But they can do it. Sometimes it takes finding out what the marketplace wants. Sometimes it takes creating brand-new wants.

This is where leadership skills make the huge difference between competitors. To survive in a competitive marketplace we must manage people who can work and create to their potential. When people work in a press, press, press environment, their creative energies are depleted. They can't think for fear of personal, professional, or corporate demise. And if people work in an environment that is always in a relaxed release mode, where there is no visionary leadership, they are not inspired to take advantage of their potential.

Of course, these last several remarks concern leading

the troops to survive in a tough market by empowering them to come up with new ideas and to deliver value to customers. Another application of the value notion concerns the value that the linkage-oriented leader brings to the employees themselves. When your people perceive that they get value from you, that their own goals can be fulfilled by working with you, they will stay with you. When they perceive that they do not derive personal value from you, they will leave — if not physically then mentally.

Linkage is the key to bringing value to your people while you bring value to yourself. Without empathy you cannot attend to their needs. Without focus, you cannot attend to your own. By finding the link between the two, it's a win/win situation.

But can it be so easy? Surely there are times when the leader must give bad news, must say "Tough, you can't have what you want" — like when the employee brings greater value and when there is no money left in the pot to give in return. Life is filled with difficult situations where the needs of all stakeholders cannot be met in one gesture.

Let's put a few situations to the test. Let's say you are the general manager of a restaurant and you have a waiter who wants to be a shift manager. You think he has a lot of rough edges — one of which is that he talks too much with the customers and is a little egocentric. He's unable to find that desired balance between being available yet not invading (that darned duality again). He thinks he's ready for the role tomorrow; you think humility is a long time coming. Your goal for the restaurant is to give the local market the white-table-cloth environment that you know it wants. The restaurant's goal is to overcome its local competition for the white-tablecloth market. The question is whether you can coach the waiter towards his goal while still fulfilling your own and the restaurant's goal. The answer is probably an easy yes.

You can communicate that he can meet his goal and that you need things from him in the process. You need him to be patient and to develop even greater finesse than he already possesses. You can explain what his finesse looks like and you can get his buy-in on how it takes time and experience. You can spend time giving examples. You can tell him that if he cannot master this goal of his in a reasonable time, then you can understand him electing to leave. You can explain that if the organization cannot bring him value, and you cannot bring him value through the education you can personally offer, if he stops deriving long-term benefit from his employ, beyond simply earning his income, then he can leave. On the other hand, you would like to make it your mission to help him reach his goal, since everybody will win from it. Also, to reach his goal, he will have to worry with you about creating new ways to differentiate the restaurant from its local competition. You can make it clear that this too is necessary for his promotion, let alone the restaurant's survival.

Let's say, though, that you believe there is no way this man can reach his goal. This makes the example somewhat more challenging. Mature managers handle this scenario predictably. With compassion, they help the person to accept reality. They support the self-esteem of the person. Then they seek to help the person anyway. They set new goals that work for both parties. And they get to work on fulfilling them.

That's what it's all about. Being focused on the well-being of the employee while moving towards goals. Dealing with the employee's reality. Working on the realistic goal fulfillment of all concerned. Being frank and compassionate. Press and release.

CONCLUSION

L ET'S take our own meta-level look at the ground we've covered. That's why we have summaries at the end of books, right? We see what we've done and we end up being better off than if we didn't get a summary.

We got rolling with a look at empathy, saying that it referred to one's ability to identify with the perspective of other people. We said that it wasn't just the patronizing effort to show that you got the gist of what other people were saying to you. Instead, it was the genuine effort to see the world from their varied points of view, and to validate those points of view. We said that empathy was critical as a management skill because it allowed you to glean other points of view and it could make your employees feel heard. It was a tool for causing their private chatter to slow down and thereby cause them to listen to you.

We moved on to put your empathy skills to the test by seeing whether you could capture the essence of an employee's point of view and run with it. Doing so would allow you to make your employees feel heard — that ever-important skill — and to optimize the chances of them hearing you as well. They would hear you because you would show that you could hear them.

And hearing you, we said, was obviously an important thing. In your role as leader, helping people to see things your way is very important. If you don't do it, we said, then you are leaving their points of view up to them, and those points of view would probably not satisfy you. What else is a leader for, we asked, if not to keep people on track towards an accepted goal or vision?

The key to making your vision clear, we said, is to empathize with your listeners. Doing so stops their chatter and thereby opens them up to your message. To do this magic of making your vision clear while empathizing with your listeners is to move between the two poles of empathy and focus while you communicate.

Not only do you communicate your vision as a leader but you have the predictable challenge of dealing with people whose self-talk tends to be problematic for you. People tend to generalize, and as a result they can get negative, taking specific occasions and generalizing them in a negative fashion. And they are troublesome to manage for other reasons as well. They can be worriers, come down hard on themselves and nurture continuous low self-esteem. They can place blame everywhere but on their own shoulders and they can uncontrollably lose their tempers. What can we do with these patterns in people's thinking? We can help them to recognize the patterns. We can enhance their self-esteem.

This took us to an important message in this book about meta-levels. We said that a meta-level was a dimension of thought that helps people to see themselves. The resulting self-awareness enables them to be objectively aware of their own behaviour and thinking style. This objective self-awareness is something we want to encourage in our employees because it empowers them to take responsibility for their mental experiences; it enables them to choose their mental events rather than be victimized by them.

All of this raised the question that if people can choose their perspectives, what perspective or mental conditions should leaders choose to sustain? Focus, we said, was a key to management success. Focused people tend to occupy themselves with goals and they tend to sustain their concentration.

When they occupy themselves with goals, they try to implement plans they make to employ resources to overcome the obstacles that hold them back from their goals. Focused people do that naturally. And they are goal oriented in all that they do. They focus on their own goals, the goals of their employees, the goals of their customers, and the goals of their organization. We are always reaching for more goals. We are always seeking to reach our goals more efficiently. It is the way business survives.

The key to being goal oriented, however, was not just in thinking about how to reach goals; it was also in being focused on attaining them. We looked at closing loops, the effort to reduce the chances of the plans we make falling by the wayside. Closing loops was a way to sustain concentration and it was as simple as keeping records or reminders. It was also considered a great way to hold people accountable.

We set goals all the time when we are focused. And we help our people to reach their own goals. We do this by coaching or developing them. Coaching is the process of helping people to reach our and their goals by working out with them a plan to do so. We said it was a key responsibility for a manager. Most of us don't do it enough, for various reasons, including that we lack the time and the knowledge of how to do it. But on the assumptions that we are focused on reaching our own goals, that we employ people to help us reach these goals, and that people usually don't have all of the skills or attitudes required to optimize the speed at which we can attain our goals, we need to coach them in order to give them the behavioural skills and self-management skills to do the job.

Along the way, we link their goals to our own goals so that managing them is a win/win situation. Indeed, helping others win while we win too seems like the best way to handle our jobs. It seems like the most socially mature thing to do. And it comes somewhat naturally to those who sustain a harmony between their own self-oriented quest and their more other-oriented, socially conscious sensibilities. The most mature leaders of all, we said, are those who make these links all the time. They operate from that place where they naturally find the common goal and satisfy all.

But it comes down to balance. A prerequisite for long-term success, either for the individual manager or for an organization as a whole, is the ability to bring value to others. Temporarily allaying self-orientation, such that one can accurately perceive the value others seek, is key. To the recipients of the gesture, it is a gift.

Imagine if we all ran around offering these gifts!

INDEX